What price glory? Heaven knows !
We're just a bunch of chums
Who're marching on to who knows where –
Until we hear the drums.

We're just the sergeant's shower. Who cares?
We take life as it comes.
And oh, the deep despondency! –
Until we hear the drums.

Browned off? I'll say. A clumsy lot
With all our fingers thumbs.
But God! we pull together when
We hear the fifes and drums.

It's all a joke! Can this be IT?
The sergeant haws and hums.
But none of us are doubting when
We hear the fifes and drums.

Thoughts are scattered, minds confused,
We dream of homes and mums.
But oh, the concentration when
We hear the bleeding drums!

Death or glory? Heroes? Us?
The truth is dawning. Crumbs!
What goads us on? What winds us up?
The bloomin

REMBRANDT VAN RIJN

Frontispiece: *'Kettledrummer' by Rembrandt (1606 – 1669). Reproduced by courtesy
of the Trustees of the British Museum.*

Hugh Barty-King

THE DRUM

A Royal Tournament
Tribute to the Military Drum

First published 1988

by The Royal Tournament,
Horse Guards, Whitehall,
London SW1A 2AX

Copyright Hugh Barty-King

ISBN 0 9513588 0 4

Designed by Keyline Creative Services, Prestwood, Bucks.

Typeset and printed by Waterlow Ltd, Dunstable, Member of BPCC plc.

CONTENTS

Then it's Tommy this, an' Tommy that, an' "Tommy ow's your soul?"
But it's "This red line of heroes when the drums begin to roll".

R. Kipling

Drum and drummer were in the centre of every British
square in Marlborough's day. The drum taps carried the
orders to the soldiers in the line and the sound of the
drumming behind them gave them the encouragement and
strength required to face and overcome the fears and
horrors of the battlefield.

From these days on the drums have remained close to
the heart of a Regiment and like Standards, Guidons and
Colours they carry the Battle Honours of the Regiment
emblazoned upon them. Today, the sound of the drum still
stirs the spirit of the soldier as it has done for four
centuries and nowhere will the drum be heard to better
effect this year than at The Royal Tournament where the
drums of twenty Regiments will be on parade.

However, in the British Army today the drummer is
also a fighting soldier and The Royal Tournament will
show him in both his roles.

Little has been written of the history of the drum
and I congratulate Mr. Hugh Barty King upon his research.
He has managed to present a great deal of information in
an easily read and entertaining form.

With this book, with the Exhibition of The Drum at
The National Army Museum and with a large part to play in
this year's Royal Tournament, Drum and Drummer will be
much in evidence in London this coming July.

H.R.H. The Duke of Kent

FOREWORD

Major General Christopher Airy, CBE
The Chairman, The Royal Tournament

I am delighted to have this opportunity to thank all those who have been associated with the research, writing, printing and publication of The Royal Tournament Book of The Drum.

It is an excellent book, most thoroughly researched, on a subject of which little has been written. This is surprising when you consider the special part that the drum has played in the history of The British Army.

With the drum as the central theme of The 1988 Royal Tournament it seemed an appropriate moment to produce this book and I have no doubt that it will prove most popular.

Due to the generous sponsorship of the book by Carrington & Co Ltd, for which I am indeed grateful, we are able to sell the first edition of the book at £3.00.

I strongly recommend to you The Book of The Drum. I am confident that you will enjoy it both as a good story and as an authoritative book of reference.

Christopher Airy

AUTHOR'S PREFACE

This is not an in-depth study of the Military Drum and its history, but a book which aims primarily to entertain, and so enlighten those who feel the urge to see and hear Corps of Drums, Marching Military Bands and Mounted Bands sounding off at the Royal Tournament. My research, though painstaking, has been far from exhaustive. More about drummers' dress, beating techniques and drill will be found in the Army's *Drummer's Handbook*. Little is known *for certain* about almost any aspect of the military drum's use in the sixteenth, seventeenth and eighteenth centuries in Britain in spite of the voluminous literature. I have plunged in with 'statements' which must be assumed to be mostly conjectural, and tried to set down the situation as far as I can make out from the writings of those, contemporary and otherwise, who have studied the subject with great care and those authorities to whom I have listened with the greatest attention.

Foremost among the latter was Mr William G F Boag, the country's leading authority on the Military Drum (and indeed on Military Music) who, until he retired in April 1988, was Assistant to the Keeper of the Scottish United Services Museum in Edinburgh Castle. I am extremely grateful to him for giving me of his time to talk to me about a subject which has been the study of a lifetime; and to others who have talked to me, particularly Mr David Leech, Chairman and Managing Director of George Potter & Co (Musical Instruments) Ltd of Aldershot; Colonel P S Walton, Chairman, The Corps of Drums Society; Mr Ian Hook, Secretary, The Corps of Drums Society; Mr Roger Davenport, Editor of the Corps of Drums Society's *Newsletter;* and Major John Tamplin of the Army Museums Ogilby Trust.

I am indebted to the correspondents who sent me valuable written information: Major Richard Powell, RAOC; Lieutenant M L A Hall (ex-RSM Coldstream Guards); Major (retd) G Horrabin, consultant to Boosey & Hawkes; Mr Roger Horrobin, Managing Director, Premier Percussion Ltd of Leicester; Mr Steve Sellwood, The Corps of Drums Society; Major (retd) J S Knight, Regimental Secretary, The Queen's Own Hussars; Major (retd) M Wright, Curator, The Royal Irish Fusiliers Museum, Armagh; and for help from Colonel Duncan Beat, Director, The Royal Military School of Music; Mr William Reid CBE, Director, The National Army Museum, London; Mrs Marian Harding and Miss Clare Wright of the National Army Museum Reading Room, and other staff, where I did most of the research; and the staffs of The British Library and The Guildhall Library, London, and of the National Library of Scotland, and the Central Reference Library, Edinburgh.

My thanks are due above all to the prime mover of this project Colonel I A Ferguson OBE, Vice-Chairman and Director of The Royal Tournament; Lieutenant Colonel A Jackson LVO, MBE, Secretary, and Lieutenant Colonel R Z Stockwell, Assistant Secretary, The Royal Tournament.

Ticehurst   H B-K

EARLY YEARS

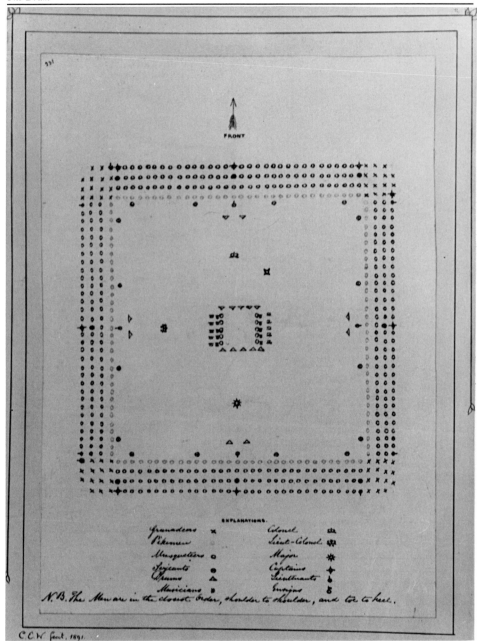

The British Square; *Colonel Clifford Walton's drawing for his* **History of the British Standing Army 1660-1700.** *The triangles show position of The Drums.*

Chapter 1

Drummer.

1   At His Captain's Heels

Beating Field Calls and Parleying in Cromwellian and Royalist regiments; the sadistic Colonel Kirke; the Ghost Drummer of Tidworth; the old English March; the Scots March; Camp Calls; Raising a Regiment; Dress for Drummers; Paint for Drums.

> **Valour and courage is necessary in all their imployments, for the Drummer's place is ever at his Captain's heeles. It is hee that brings the Battels to joyne, hee that stands in the midst when swords flie on all sides; hee that brings them to pell mell and the furie of execution; and it is hee that brings them both on and off, when they are either fortunate or abandoned or forsaken.**

> Francis Markham, *Five Decades of Epistles of Warre*

That was how it happened on paper. On the field of battle the two drummers assigned to the captain of a seventeenth century company of musketeers and pikemen would not be at his heels as he led his men from the front, sword in hand, pell mell against the enemy. By then they had joined the drummers of the other nine companies, and the colonel's drummer, in the command post in the centre of the regiment. There stood the standard bearer with the regimental flag – the Colours. From there the colonel controlled the movement of the captain-led companies in front of him. In the heat of the moment he may have tried shouting his commands to the wind, but his voice would never have carried to the men in the line. A better way was to give his order to the non-commissioned officer who stood beside him and the Colours, the Regimental Drum-Major who then passed the order on to the 21 drummers who beat it out according to a prescribed code.

Not every regiment had a drum-major at this time. Gerat Barry referred to one in the *Militarie Discipline* he wrote in 1634. Sir John Hepburn certainly had one in his regiment in 1637. In rank he was somewhere between on NCO and a commissioned officer. In *The Soldier's Grammar* of 1639 he is rated as superior to a sergeant. He was not a proper adjunct of a regiment until 1659 however. Himself a proficient side-drummer, his job was to appoint, train and superintend the regiment's side-drummers.

Before the actual head-on clash, considerable time was spent on manoeuvering the men into their battle positions. To alert them that the climax of all their training was imminent and they were on the point of being called upon to *fight*, the captain had his two drummers beat a Call. His training had told each infantry-man that these beats meant that, wherever he was, he was to stop what he was doing and go at once to his ensign – the lieutenant, his 'platoon commander'. He must listen out for another urgent command to follow shortly.

The captain thereupon told his drummers to beat a Troop which told his men to 'shoulder your muskets, advance your pikes, to close your ranks and files to the place of rendezvous'; and then a March 'by which you are to understand to take your open order in rank, to shoulder both muskets and pikes, and to direct your march, either quicker or slower, according to the beat of the drum'.

The captain's final order by a beat from the two company drummers at his heels was a Preparative: 'close to your due distance for skirmish both in rank and file, and make ready that you may execute upon the first command.' Another military manual writer of the period Captain Thomas Venn described the sequence.

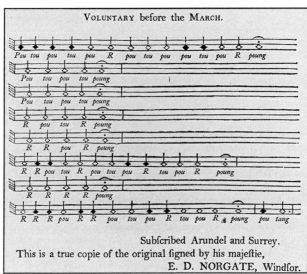

English
March
1632

VOLUNTARY before the MARCH.

Pou tou pou tou pou R pou tou pou pou tou pou R poung

Pou tou pou tou poung

Pou tou pou tou poung

R pou tou R poung

R R pou R poung

R R pou tou R pou tou pou R tou pou R poung

R R R R poung

R R R pou R R pou tou pou R tou pou R poung pou tang

Subfcribed Arundel and Surrey.
This is a true copie of the original figned by his majeftie,
E. D. NORGATE, Windfor.

A Company of Foot being thus drawn up for service and the Colours flying in the head of the Company, and there they are to remain until all forlorne [advance party] firings are ended. But so soon as the Drumm[er] shall beat his further preparatives for a close skirmish, the Ensigne is to furle his colours and retreat to the half files of pikes.

At that point the company drummers ran to where the colonel stood, or sat on his horse, beside his own side-drummer and the standard bearer. When all was ready, the colonel gave his drum-major the order to beat a Battaile or Charge which Colonel William Barriffe described as meaning 'pressing forward in order of battaile without lagging behind, rather boldly stepping forward in place of him that falls dead or wounded before thee.' The 21 drummers beat it out with a roar which, apart from being clearly audible and instantly interpreted, hopefully gave them the courage to face the ordeal which lay ahead and instilled terror into the enemy opposite.

Barriffe maintained that after the Charge had been beaten the drum was still 'the voice of the commander, the spurre of the valiant and the heart of the coward.' By it, he said, the soldiers must receive their directions 'when the roaring cannon, the clashing of armies, the neighing of horses and other confused noise caused neither captain nor other officer can be heard.' To Thomas Venn too 'it is when by reason of a great noise of Guns, men and armes and horses, the commander's voice can neither he heard or obey'd without the beat of a drum, the action of the souldier, whether valiant or otherwise, is to be guided by it.' But the din, which included the screams of the wounded and the firing of the muskets, is likely to have made it impossible for the men to have heard even the drum beats. However, when the colonel saw from his vantage point beside the Colours that the time had come for 'an orderly retiring backward, either for relief, for advantage of ground, for some other political end as to draw the enemy into some ambushment', he called to his drum-major to have his drummers beat a Retreat.

Though military operations in the seventeenth century were comparatively uncomplicated – hence the need for only six basic orders – they were highly confusing. If a regiment was to carry out the tactical plan conceived by its commander, which he hastily had to change as circumstances dictated, it was essential that each infantryman fighting for his life was able, without the slightest hesitation, to recognise the regulated drum beat above the uproar and bedlam yet to reach its climax. Thomas Venn insisted on every soldier 'endeavouring to know the several Beates of the Drum, or he may often fall short of the captain's commands.' The military signs for the soldier to walk, or guide his actions by, were termed 'Semivocall Signes', he said. It was the captain's duty 'to teach his souldiers distinctly the several beats of the Drum that they may be the better able to perform their respective duties whenever they shall be commanded by the drum.'

Each beat had to be plain and distinctive – incapable of being taken for another.

For the drummer it was a great responsibility. Francis Markham was in no two minds about the drummer's importance. He was

> **the very tongue and voyce of the Commander. He is to have an exceeding careful and diligent ear into all the wordes of directions (and are called *Vocabula Artis*) which shall proceede from the Captain, and accordingly to performe and speake it in his beatings.**
>
> **For to mistake and do contrary as to beat a Retrait when he is commanded to Charge, or to beat a Charge when men are to Retire, were a thing of that danger that the armie might perish by the action.**

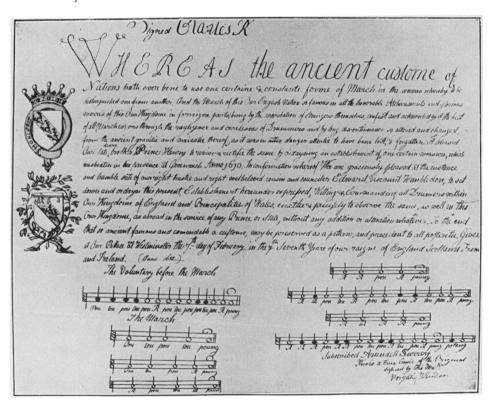

Warrant for The English March 1632.

To reduce the chance that a drummer would make so dire a mistake, the captain had to be at pains 'to instruct and inform soldiers and make plain to them the alteration of notes and how they differ in their significations.' In his turn the illiterate recruit had to be prepared to have drummed into him ad nauseam the beatings considered 'the most behoveful and useful'. The key to the drum's ability to transmit the captain's or colonel's orders was crisp, short simplicity. The drummer must not be tempted to show off, to add frills of his own, to demonstrate his virtuosity. 'Let therefore the Drummer studie Art and Plainnesse, for that is the best to draw a dull mind to apprehension.' He should be left to play his responsible role unmolested. A drummer was 'more a man of peace than of the sword; and it was most dishonourable in any man (willingly and out of his knowledge) to strike or wound him'.

It is most necessary that the Drumme[r] and Phiphe[r] bee men of verie able and praise worthie qualities, and of comely and well-shaped proportions and indued with all these especiall Vertues which should adorne a perfect Souldier as Obedience, Silence, Secrecie, Sobrietie, Valour and Loyaltie, that so they may bee the great Examples of duetie to those which shall live about them; close in all Counsels, Temperate in delivering messages, Stout in performing the will of their Commaunders, the faithfull in all their undertakings; all of which will bee as so many Crownes and Garlands to adorne their good deeds; and by that meanes Vertue will never forsake them, nor will true Reward and Merit lose a Purchase it hath got with so much honour.

Side-drummers and fifer, funeral of Sir Philip Sidney 1587.

The importance of a drummer delivering messages temperately was second only to his accuracy in beating the orders of his commander. He was chosen for the job of drummer not only for 'the exqusiteness and skilfulness in his Art and Instrument' but for his aptitude in 'parleying', going across to the enemy lines and acting as a go-between. To do this he had to be a person who was naturally discreet, and did not drink too much ale 'so that he circumvented others rather than himself be circumvented'. He had to be cunning and careful on entering the enemy's camp to observe warily their works, guards and sentinels, and be able to give an account of them when he returned. He had to be able to read and write, which was more than most privates could do, so was socially their superior. Not only that, he had to be a good linguist 'and well seene in forraine languages'. His ignorance of the other side's tongue would make him a servant when he should dominate the situation as the master of it. A drummer who walked into the enemy den less than fearlessly, and faltered in his words of address, would be despised and run the risk of instant execution, his dismembered body being ignominiously returned to his commander packed into the wooden shell of his drum.

He has to carry Ransomes and pay agreements between his Side and the Enemie. It is hee that must trucke and compound for prisoners. Hee must bring them home when redeemed and place them in safety. He must conduct pledges, carry them and re-carry them, and leade to the enemy and his own tente such hostages and prisoners as shall be exchanged; and carry Challenges and Defiances from one enemie to another.

Not every enemy took kindly to a challenge, and the man who delivered it had to be every inch a diplomat. For that reason, said Robert Ward in his *Animadversions of Warre* (1639), a drummer was 'one of the necessariest officers to a company'. 'Divers passages of waight and moment hee is to be employed in, for many times they are sent to parlie with the enemie.' On such occasions he should carry a small drum for lightness and 'also to have a paper wherein is writ the Contents of his Message which is to Placed upon his Hatte'.

When he approaches neere the Enemies Towne hee is to make a stand a Musquet-shot from the Ports [gates], and to beate a Parley whereby they may know his intent. Hee ought to be of a singular good carriage and discreet, to observe and take notice of all passages; that may give any intelligence to his officers of the State of the Enemie. Hee must be very wary that nothing be screwd from him, neither by fayre or foule meanes; wherefore he must be wary of the Enemies friendship in bestowing courtesies upon him especially in giving him drinke, least in his cupps he reveale any secrets.

Likewise when a drummer was received in the camp from the enemy's side he had to be handled with the greatest caution.

Drummer, First or Royal Regiment of Foot Guards, 1660

Illustrations by Clifford Walton for his History of the British Standing Army 1660 – 1700 *(1894) in the Library of the Royal United Services Institute, London, by whose kind permission they are reproduced.*

Drummer and Musqueteer Private, The Thirteenth Foot, 1692.

Kettledrum carriage of The Royal Artillery, with fifer and side-drummer, beside the River Roer in the Low Countries in 1748. Painting by David Morier in the National Army Museum on loan from the Royal Collection and reproduced by gracious permission of Her Majesty the Queen.

Hee must not be suffered to approach near the guards nor the ports untill an Officer bee sent into him (who must be attended with a guard of Musquetires) and having blind-folded him. He is to be conducted into the Campe to the General's Pavilion where a guard must pass on him least he should discover the weaknesse of the Camp.

Number VIII of Robert Ward's Articles of War was headed 'Speaking with the Enemies Messengers': 'None shall speak with a Drum or Trumpet or any other sent by the Enemy without order upon pain of punishment at discretion.'

It was touch and go for the drummer whom the royalist Governor of Sherborne Castle, 'having cooled his brain with a little sleep', dispatched at two in the morning on Friday August 15 1645 with a message that he was willing to surrender upon honourable terms. When he read the Governor's message Sir Thomas Fairfax, Captain General of all the Parliamentary Forces in England, was hard put to it to keep his temper.

'Answer was returned' recorded Joshua Sprigge in *Anglia Rediviva* (1647) 'no terms but Quarter, seeing he had slipt and slighted the opportunity; and he was not to expect that, except he rend'red speedily.'

This was a near-insult. And the Governor's resentment was exacerbated by the way in which the message was delivered. Fairfax's drummer was over-confident. The Governor of Sherborne Castle thought his demeanour was too saucy by a half and threatened to hang him. Maybe the drummer had been told of Sir James Turner's advice in *Pallas Armata* that 'if drummers can carry a message wittily to the enemy they may be permitted to be drolls', and had over-stepped the mark.

He was allowed to return to Fairfax's headquarters however, whereupon the general went himself to the earthworks and had a look at the inside of the castle over the wall 'not without great hazard'. He then ordered his troops to storm it. Every soldier was to cut his fresh faggot. In six hours they had six thousand faggots to fill the trenches with, and threw stones and rubbish on them. All was noise and bustle.

Trumpets on turrets high,
These are a-sounding;
Drums beating out aloud,
Echoes resounding;
Alarm bells in each place,
They are a-ringing;
Women with stones in their laps
To the walls bringing.

When cannons are roaring
And bullets are flying,
He that would honour win
Must not fear dying.

When there was no longer any chance of winning honour, which John Forbes, the author of the above, and his contemporaries saw as an end in itself, whatever the cause they were meant to be fighting for, there was only one course left, as Anne Finch reflected when the costly civil strife was over.

Trail all your pikes, dispirit every drum,
March in long procession from afar
Ye silent, ye dejected men of war!
Be still the hautboys, let the flute be dumb!

For many the detached drum beat in battle, unafffected by the heart-rending sounds of human suffering around it, acquired an ethereal quality—a spirit of its own. For them it helped to dull the senses to the horrific reality of it all. But for the sadistic Colonel Piercy Kirke it was a means of making death even less endurable. Charged with the duty of rounding up the followers of the king's defeated bastard the Duke of Monmouth after their defeat at the Battle of Sedgemoor, Kirke had 19 prisoners hanged in front of him as soon as he entered Bridgewater, without bothering to establish their complicity by a trial. According to David Hume (whom modern historians of the Queen's Royal Regiment, which Kirke's Regiment became, accuse of undue bias however).

Observing their feet to quiver in the agonies of death, he
[Kirke] cried that he would give them music to their dancing,
and he immediately commanded the drums to beat and the
trumpets to sound.

Hume stated that the colonel had served in Tangiers and 'had contracted an inhumanity from his intercoure with the Moors less known in European and free countries'.

Fiendish use of the drum such as this perhaps inspired what Samuel Pepys wrote of in his diary—'the present appearing of the Devil in Wiltshire much of late talked of who beats a drum up and down. "The Devil" do answer to any tune that you will play upon another drum, yet one time he tried to play it and could not.'

The occurrence was the subject of conversation at a dinner which Pepys was having with some friends. Lord Sandwich, who was one of the guests, said he thought the failure to repeat the tune on that occasion seemed to make the whole thing suspect, and Samuel agreed with him. Someone called Joseph Glanville wrote a pamphlet entitled *A Relation of the famed disturbance at the house of Mr Mompesson at Tedworth, Wilts, occasioned by the beating of an invisible drum every night for a year.* The story was widely believed at the time, but a conclusive piece of investigative journalism by the *Mercurius Publicus* revealed it to be a hoax and the 'invisible drummer'

CCXLIV

C. C. W. fecit, 1867.

Punishment of the Gatloupe.
Seventeenth and Eighteenth centuries.

CCXLIII

to be one William Drury of the Wiltshire village of Uscut. In the next century Joseph Addison made it the subject of a play he called *The Drummer, or the Haunted House* (1792) in which the principal characters were Fantome The Drummer and Vellum Sir George Truman's Steward. The 'ghost drumming' was a device to cover milady's illicit amours. After the final curtain the speaker of the Epilogue asked the audience

> *No court intrigue, nor city cuckoldom,*
> *No song, no dance, no music—but a drum—*
> *No smutty thought in doubtful phrase exprest,*
> *And gentlemen, if so, pray where's the jest?*

On at least one occasion a hoax drumming was used as a military tactic to deceive the enemy into believing it represented the presence of a large body of men. After some hours spent during a night in March 1642 attacking the town of Malmesbury, the Parliamentary leader Sir William Waller found he had run out of ammunition and had better withdraw. But how to do so without having the royalists turn his retreat into a rout? 'To prevent the hazard of the enemy's sally I caused all the drums to beat and the trumpets to sound'. Under the brou-ha-ha of his drummers' furious beating Waller managed to break off the engagement unscathed and make an orderly retreat. Moreover the royalists, believing the great volume of sound indicated an imminent attack by a force of overwhelming size, sent a drummer to Waller beating a parley. Malmesbury was surrendered to him at seven o'clock the next morning, without a shot being fired by troops full of sound and fury which, to the dismay of the town's bamboozled defenders, had signified nothing. And that was no jest either.

If the ghostly drum beats made Sir George Truman's blood run cold, and deterred him from hunting down his wife's lover, the beatings of earth-bound company drummers played on the emotions of infantrymen of the line in a more stimulating way by giving them a rhythm to walk to and make the lengthy tramping less laborious. Next in importance to signalling was the drum's role as an aid to marching.

The roads of seventeenth century England were atrocious. For the most part they were merely tracks which made 'marching' impossible. Infantry regiments slogged slowly along them in undisciplined lumps at some 75 to 90 paces a minute, and there was no attempt to accompany them with drum beats. Rain forced them to go even more slowly. Reporting to the Speaker of the House of Commons on the Battle of Preston in the summer of 1648 Oliver Cromwell told him how

> **we lay that night in the field close by the enemy, being very dirty and weary, and having marched twelve miles of such ground as I never rode in all my life, the day being very wet.**

Nearer a town the track became firmer, and the beating of drums would bring the struggling foot soldiers to attention so they could form up into some semblance of marching order. They then proceeded into the town to the beat of the drum—though probably not in step. That was reserved for parades and formal drill movements.

Dignity and gravity were said to characterise the way English foot regiments proceeded from one camp to another to the drum beat known as the Old English March. It contrasted with the French March which had the reputation of being brisk and alert. A French general, Maréchal Biron, once told an army officer in the days of Queen Elizabeth I, Sir Roger Williams, that he considered the English March, being beaten by a drum, 'slow, heavy and sluggish'. 'That may be so' relied Sir Roger, 'but slow as it is, it has crossed your master's country from one end to the other.'

By the beginning of the seventeenth century this Old English March of the 16th, and perhaps an earlier, century had become corrupted by players whose private 'arrangements' were far removed from the original. Performers such as these were perhaps the target of Francis Markham's barbed observations in his *Five Decades* (1622):

> **Neither ought a man to be (like Captain Hindar) so nice and curious in the beatings of the Drumme, proportioning the body, legges, head and hands and every motion so exactly to every stroke or doubling of the Drumme, as if it were almost a treason in Nature to walke without that Instrument's assistance.**

Efforts were made therefore to recover the English March and re-introduce it in its original form as the standard for all regiments of the line. 'I have thought meete for the benefit of each drummer which is not yet perfect in the March' wrote the anonymous author of *Warlike Directions* (1643),

> **to pricke down the old English March newly revived in the plainest forme I could invent. Wishing that all Drummers would leave off other forms invented, either by themselves or others herein unskillful, that there may be uniformitie in this Kingdome, as in all other nations.**

Charles I was keen to see the Old English March revived, and in 1632 issued a warrant, endorsed by his Earl Marshal the Earl of Arundel and Surrey, directing lord lieutenants of counties to make sure it was. It had been the ancient custom of nations, ran the preamble, to use one certain and constant form of march in wars so that one side's could be distinguished from the other's. The English March 'so famous in all honourable achievements and glorious warres of this our kingdome in forraigne parts' had been acknowledged by strangers to be the best of all marches. However 'through the negligence and carelessnesse of drummers and by long discontinuance' it had become so altered and changed from its ancient gravity and majesty as to have been in danger of becoming lost and forgotten. What was considered the proper measure had been beaten in the presence of Prince Henry at Greenwich in 1610. The king now ordained that all drummers in England and Wales were to observe this measure exactly and precisely, both inside the kingdom and abroad in the service of any foreign prince or state, 'without any addition or alteration whatsoever, to the end that so antient, famous and commendable a custome may be preserved as a patterne and precedent to all posteritie.'

The warrant contained a notation of the 'Voluntary before the March' on three staves forming an upper and a lower row. The diamond-shaped notes were all on the lower row and some were solid black and others open. Underneath each note was an onomatopoeic 'word': pou, tou, poung or tang, or the letter R. No one knows what they were intended to convey.

But the drummers who took part in the tournament which William Barriffe described in *Mars His Triumph* must have known what they meant. It was a mock battle between English infantry and soldiers dressed up as 'Saracens'. It was staged inside a hall in front of an audience of the nobility and City of London aldermen.

> **Grave fathers of the City that are come,**
> **Like the fam'd senators of ancient Rome**
> **From seats of Justice and the Publicke cause**
> **To hear Bellona's drums beat loud applause.**

The Exercise with a grand procession headed by the 'Saracens'. 'Lastly Captain John Ven led-in the Modern Armes, his Drumes beating a lofty English Martch, his souldiers being but 32 in number, he could martch two abreast.'

The noise would have excited the audience of this staged spectacle as it did those who gathered to witness the real-life drama of the raising of the King's standard at Nottingham in 1642 when Clarendon, historian of the Great Rebellion, had it that 'there was very little other ceremony than the sound of drums and trumpets'.

Revival of the English March did little to speed up the transfer of foot regiments—Charles took ten days to move his army the 100 miles from Shrewsbury to Banbury—but it will have made a better impression.

There was a separate Scots March, the nature of which has given rise to considerable speculation. It was national and not partisan, and in his *Songs and Marches of the Roundheads and Cavaliers* Lewis Winstock thinks it was probably played indiscriminately by the Scots armies that aided the Parliamentarians in 1644 and those that fought for the Royalists at Preston, Dunbar and Worcester. Samuel Pepys heard the Royal Scots beat 'Dumbarton's Drums' in the streets of Rochester in June 1667 'which is very odd'. He considered it to be the Scots March and the oldest march in existence. There is an unconfirmed tradition that it was composed in 1527 during the seige of Tantallon Castle when James V of Scotland got the best of the rebellious Archibald Douglas. Winstock believes it to have been the march of the Scots Brigade who fought for the Protestants in the Thirty Years War. 'It was played at Leipzig in 1631 when Robert Monro sounded it in the dust and smoke of battle so that his position should be known to both friend and foe.' It was still the regimental air of the First of Foot as late as 1679.

Accounts such as that by Pepys and others that the Scots March was 'beat' should indicate it was a one-note rhythm for drums, but the *air* of more than one note in Elizabeth Rogers's manuscript Virginal Book of 1656, which Dr Henry Farmer believes was the Scots March, must have been played by pipes or flutes (fifes) with or without drums, but not by drums alone. This was *music* which the monotone beat of an untunable military side-drum was not—any more than the buzz of a telegraph key. A side-drummer did not normally 'play' from written music such as that reproduced in the 1632 warrant. He learnt his beats off by heart—by rote. First he learnt the rudiments—a 'flam' which was an extended stroke preceded by a light stroke; a 'roll' which was a continuous beating with both sticks. How quickly flams and rolls were beaten in the seventeenth century is anyone's guess; how long a roll was, whether it was repeated, whether it was just plop-plop or plop-plop purr. Having mastered the rudiments he was taught how to put them together into a Call. Field Calls, as seen, were few and infrequent but vital. More numerous and more frequently beaten were the Camp or Duty Calls.

TWO "DRUMMS AND A FIFE AND THE DRUMME-MAJOR."
F. Sandford, "Funeral of the Duke of Albemarle," 1670.

These were distinguished from what Thomas Venn called the Poynts of War by being not so much Signalled Commands as Time Checks. They acted as the Camp Clock. They divided up the soldier's day, announced the sequence of events in camp or garrison, just as the school bell told everyone what they were expected to do next in the classroom or on the playing field.

At the beginning of each day a drum beat gave the soldier a morning call to wake up and get up; at the end of it another told him to stop tippling and return to camp. 'A Revally is beaten in the morning by daylight' stated Venn in 1622, 'at which time the sub officers are to take off their sentinels' who had been posted at sunset the previous day with a different Camp Call. 'The Ta-to beaten' he said, 'when the Watch is set at the discretioin of the Governour, after which in most places or Garrisons of note there is a warning piece discharged so that none are to be out of their houses without the word is given them.'

At the end of the previous century, Robert Barret had described (in his *Theorike and Practice of Modern Warres* 1598) how a the right time the Captain 'shall call together the company which should be of the watch, the which are to be advertised thereof from the morning by the Drumme Major of the regiment, and he is then to set them in their places', a routine which still prevailed. The Call beaten at this point was probably the Field Call of the Retreat which had somehow come to be used also as a Camp Call.

The Officer of the Watch or Picquet Officer then set off to inspect each sentinel to make sure he had been posted in the right place, was awake and knew his duties. His first encounter was the sentinel at the First Post, and the drummer he had with him beat a Call to tell the sentinel at the next post that the officer was on his way. The tour of inspection took about half an hour and ended at sunset at the Last Post, at which the officer's drummer beat the Tattoo telling everyone the watch was set and warned soldiers outside that in a quarter of an hour or so the gates (if there were any) would be shut, and that anyone seeking to enter the camp or garrison would be challenged by an armed sentinel.

At the same time as the watch was being set, side-drummers, probably accompanied by fifers, paraded the streets of the town also sounding a Tattoo (also referred to as a Retreat) to make sure the tavern keepers knew the time had come for them to bid their military customers drink up, refuse to serve them any more ale and encourage them to make their way back to camp without spending time on further tippling. The drummers in the camp or on the garrison walls might 'answer' their comrades on the streets and themselves beat a Tattoo, after they had beaten it officially at the Last Post.

The Tattoo enjoined the publican to turn off his ale taps. Th word was a corruption of the Dutch phrase *Die den tap toe!*, picked up when English regiments were fighting in the Netherlands (the 'Low Countries'), which meant just that— 'turn off your taps!'.

No soldier could fire his musket after the sentinel had been placed at the Last Post and the camp had been closed for the night, unless he was a sentinel. Much of his day was spent however in being trained how to handle it, on musket drill and pike drill—and he did this to the beat of the drum.

'When the company is drawing up, the Drum is beat a Troop, the Pike to be advanced, the Musquets to be poised and, being in a body, are ready for command'. The display of musketry at the tournament described by William Barriffe was regulated by beat of drum.

'The second time of their coming into the Hall the Drums beat a Troop, the Pikes advance and the Rank close forward . . . where being at a distance convenient, they make a stand and the Drums strike an Alt and are silent' The pikemen and musketeers were divided into three groups 'to make them fit to keep time with the Drum and Phife' who played The Posture Tune. Postures began with Poyse your musquets ! and followed on with Open your pans and cleer !, Charge with bullet !, Shorten your scouring sticks ! Cock your matches ! Give fire brest-high! and the rest. When the men had gone through all 24 postures, the drummers and fifers played the Falling Off Tune. After a rest to recover their breath, Drums and Fifes struck up the Almain Tune for the men to do Motions. At the end of it all there was the inevitable heroic Epilogue.

> **Unbrace your drums and let the Warlike Phife**
> **No more distinguish 'twixt pale Death and Life;**
> **Furle up your Engines, let the Cannon cease**
> **And re-assume your (bravely purchast) Peace.**

The 'Turks' became Christian again 'leaving that course of life, and are now either merchants or shop-keepers for the most part.'

How best to stimulate a latent leaning towards a military life which lasted longer than an afternoon's tournament disguised as the Enemy was the problem of every gentleman who sought to raise a regiment of his own. But there was one medium he knew would never fail. The noise of a drum being beaten at the market cross always aroused attention, and its stirring rataplan could always be relied upon to conjure up the necessarily romantic picture of soldiering which was the goal of every Recruiting Sergeant. When a man like Sir John Hepburn received permission in 1633 to raise a regiment for service under the King of France his warrant authorised him to enlist volunteers 'by Beat of Drum or otherwise'. If the colonel was a southerner the warrant might give special privileges if he came looking for volunteers in the City of London.

> **This is to authorise and permitt the bearer thereof to beat up**
> **Drums within the Citty of London towards levyeing of forces**
> **for to goe in his Majesty's Service under the command of the**
> **Earl of Teviott to Tangeire without any lett or molestation.**

The traditional right to march through the streets of the capital with drums beating, colours flying and bayonets fixed was at this time claimed only by The Buffs, the Royal Marines, the London Militia and The Honourable Artillery Company.

That Captain John Mordaunt with the above warrant was raising forces *for his Majesty's service* shows the occasion was after the return of the exiled King Charles from Holland and the formation in England of the regiments from which sprang the Regular Army of to-day. The loyalty of military drummers, along with that of every infantryman, could now be said to be to the King rather than merely to his commanding officer and his faction.

In 1656 King Charles had formed his own Royal Regiment of Guards in Bruges under Colonel Lord Wentworth, and this had seven drummers—three in the King's Company, two in the Colonel's Company and two in another company. They were paid twelve pence a day. They accompanied him on his journey back home in May 1660.

Oliver Cromwell's New Model Army was disbanded except for some former Parliamentary soldiers who were deputed to man the kingdom's 28 fortresses under royalist offices. General Monk was allowed to keep his Coldstream Regiment which had effected the Restoration, and his own regiment of horse. When Monk's Regiment had moved from Coldestream on the Tweed to London they marched to the 'unofficial' drums and fifes of Fenwick's and Hasilrige's Companies playing the Highlander's March ('General Monk's Right March'). The regiment's drummers had been reduced to ten in 1657 (and no drum-major). In 1660 however it had 21, and their rolls and flams welcomed the Merry Monarch in support of Monk at Dover.

A second Royal Regiment of Guards was formed, this time in England, in November 1660 with three drummers in the King's Company and two each in the Colonel's, the Lieutenant Colonel's and Major's Company, and two each in eight other companies—25 in all at 12d a day. They had to wait till October 1661 for a drum-major who was paid 1s 6d a day (two guineas a month). In 1665, when Lord Wentworth died, the two regiments were incorporated as a single unit of 24 companies, The First Regiment of Foot Guards, with a drum-major and 36 drummers.

Monk's Coldstream Regiment had become the Lord General's Regiment of Foot in the service of the Crown in February 1661, and The Militia, which had been formed in 1641, was made a constitutional force for the defence of the realm with its own drummers who, with the privates and NCOs, were relied uon to feed what was now the 'regular' army. Other drummers at the time of the Restoration were in the ranks of the many mercenary regiments of the old kind, who were still serving masters in foreign parts oblivious of the great change which the events of 1660 had brought to the establishment of the Army in the mother country.

When a regular regiment of the line went overseas it had a larger establishment, which meant taking on more drummers than it had in the depot at home. In 1680 the establishment of The Buffs Regiment was 40 officers, 24 sergeants, 36 corporals, 12 drummers and 600 privates. When they mustered for foreign service in

Flanders in 1692 they more than doubled their number of drummers to 26. On their return to England in 1698 after the Peace of Ryswick their strength was reduced to ten companies with one drummer each.

Before they went to Flanders privates and drummers of The Buffs were dressed the same way in red uniforms lined with cloth the colour of ash wood—buff. They had breeches and stockings of the same colour. But in 1693 privates were given grey coats and breeches, and the drummers purple coats and grey breeches. The new uniform for drummers was more costly than a private's, and only a few shillings less than a sergeant's. Moreover a drummer in The Buffs wore a feather in his hat which added another shilling to the total cost of £3 15s 6d, plus a drummer's badge at 3s 6d. Both privates and drummers of The Buffs wore a loose extra sleeve hanging from the shoulder up to 1660, but thereafter it was only worn by drummers and trumpeters who took pride in it as their swagger distinguishing mark. It was later hooked up to the waistband and ornamented with lace.

The finery of the drummer spilt over on to his drum. It became the fashion to have the regimental crest, the colonel's arms or the royal arms emblazoned on the wooden side of a drum. The Royal Regiment of Guards were given permission to paint their new drums when they returned from France in 1662 on the strength of a warrant which can still be seen. It was a trend which reflected the end of the austerity of the drably dressed, sober minded Puritans whose military music was confined to hymn tunes. When Lord Maidstone, son of the Earl of Winchelsea, raised a regiment in Kent in 1668 he had crests painted on each of his three drums. An order of 1670 was for 'three drums with badges' to be issued to troops at York. The body of the drum of the Volunteer Corps, raised in Oxford in 1685 to guard roads in Berkshire and Wiltshire at the time of the Monmouth Rebellion, was royal blue with scarlet rims strung with white cord, and bore the arms of the company commander Leopold Finch, a Fellow of All Souls. When the Corps was disbanded the drum was deposited in All Souls where it still lies. Any more elaborate emblazoning however was reserved for the next century.

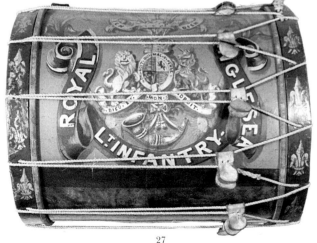

Emblazoned kettledrums: **above** *17 c;* **below** *19th c – from Potters.*

Chapter 2

2 Tabours and Nakers

Copying the Turks; first military use; Drums and Fifes in Tudor England; Drum-Major-General appoints, Drum-Major instructs—and flogs the regiment's offenders; Mounted kettledrummers for the Cavalry, Kettledrums in Carriages for the Artillery; Fifes lose popularity for 50 years from 1695.

That a drum should be decorative as well as effective was perhaps a throw-back to the time when, having for long made folk music for private dancing accompanied by a whistle, it became an aristocratic status symbol. Its size and magnificence, when beaten in a nobleman's retinue, notified all who stood and gaped of the degree of respect which was due to him. It was there to impress, not to be danced to, let alone to signal or set the time of day. It was a ceremonial toy not military equipment. And the more there were of them in the train, the louder the noise, the greater the awe.

The first people in Britain to hear the drum used in that way outside the barns and taverns, were the cheering crowds watching the lord of the manor or maybe the king go by, surrounded by a retinue whose colourful tunics and flags dazzled their eyes, whose drum beating deafened their ears.

Grafted on to the crude drum of the barndance was the more sophisticated instrument beaten by the warriors of Araby for more sinister reasons. When 30 years after the Norman Conquest of England, the West was called upon by Pope Urban II to take up arms and recover the holy places in Jerusalem from the heathen Arabs, the English nobility seized the opportunity to gain the promised remission of their sins—and escape from their families and their debts—and joined the Pope's Crusade in their hundreds. In Palestine they found that the armies of their infidel enemies the Saracens—as they called all muslims (after the Latin word for Arab)—were using drums in a way that had never occurred to them, and of a design that was new to them.

In French, which was the language of the ruling class in England after 1066, the word for this kind of small drum, some ten inches in diameter, was 'naccaire', a corruption of the Arabic *naggara*. Many of the English crusaders who managed to return home alive brought a couple of captured naccaires with them as a souvenir. They were soon calling them nakers. Others had laid hands on the smaller Persian variety whose name *taburak* they turned into tabor or tabour. These were made of double-headed, rope-tensioned sheep or calf skin, held to the side in one hand and played with a single wooden stick by the other. It was the prototype of the side-drum; and the naker, suspended in front of the player near his groin by a strap round the waist or from the shoulder, of the kettledrum (of which more later).

More tabours and nakers were brought back to England by knights who returned from the series of crusades that followed, the last of which ended in 1291 with the Christians being driven out of Syria. They adopted the fashion of the Saracens of having a servant beating a tabour or a naker as part of a personal retinue.

The man who took precedence over all others in England, the king, seized on the Saracen novelty to give his entourage the added lustre which he knew he would find at the courts of his fellow monarchs in Europe. Tabourers beat with great effect at the Great Feast which King Edward I held in Westminster Hall in 1306. In 1310 his incapable and indolent son Edward II, in need of a gimmick to bolster his authority, hired an oriental Janino le Nakerer as his minstrel and drummer boy. Edward III followed suit by appointing one Lambekin Taborer to the royal household. When in 1370, after that long siege, he finally took possession of Calais, he entered with 'a foison de trompettes, tabours, nacaires et buccines'.

Soon the sound of the tabour was being used not only to heighten the pageantry of victory parades but help achieve the victory itself. Early in the 14th century Edward III brought it into play *during* battle, along with well-orchestrated cries, to strike terror into the foe. A ballad describing Edward's victory over the Scots at Hallidown Hill told how he won it 'with merry sound'.

with pipes, trumpes and tabers thereto,
And loud clariones thei blew also.

A prose account of the same battle reported:

then the Englische mynstrelles beaten their tabers and blewen their trumpes, and pipers pipedene loude, and made a great chowte upon the Skottes.

And the noise was intended not only to demoralise the Scots but strengthen the resolve of the English. For it indicated that so long as the fighters could hear the drums beating around their commander, then the 'Colours', the centre of resistance in battle, had not been captured and, if they fought resolutely on, victory could still be theirs.

This had been the role of the drums for the Arabs. As Dr Henry Farmer, leading authority on the subject has written—though not everyone to-day takes his conclusions as reliable as once they were held to be:

So long as the Saracenic *tabl khana* (military band) was heard playing, the Muslims fought on, since it was only the absolute cessation of this music that indicated that the colours were lost as were furled in retreat, and that the battle was over. All our books in English on military discipline . . . show the music and the colours linked together in a similar manner to that of the Saracens.

In Islamic armies the seizing of the drums was a disgrace; the capture of the other side's drums a great glory—and so it became in fourteenth century England. To this very day a British regiment which has had its colours or drums taken by the enemy is not allowed to replace them easily. For it meant that the enemy had penetrated right to the guts of the regiment which had not only been defeated but routed. When the time came for the presentation of new colours or new drums it was done with religious ceremonial.

Walking kettledrum 1685.

31

The English word 'tabor' was dropped in the sixteenth century in favour of 'drome', 'droume' or 'drume' (a contraction of the more cumbrous drumslade)—an obvious onomatopoeic representation of the noise it made when beaten, akin to 'rum' the word given to the drink which provoked noisy, rumbustious behaviour by those who drank too much of it. The Elizabethan historian Stow described the flamboyant march of the London Train-Bands from Mile End to Westminster in 1539 as being accompanied by 'droumes and fyffers', dressed in canvas doublet, coloured hat, Venetian hose of Kentish broadcloth, Kersey stockings and leather shoes. The Robert Brewer who was appointed to Henry VIII's household was designated Master *Drummer.* In a book by Bishop Joseph Hall (born 1574) was the phrase 'and sodainly strake up a Dromme or Drounslade'. By the end of the sixteenth century, when William Shakespeare wrote his play *Henry IV,* the spelling had settled down. He had Falstaff discoursing on the type of men he had pressed into army service and asserting that he always steered clear of 'warm slaves as had lieve hear the devil as a drum'.

The best inn or lodging was to be provided for the Captain, stated a treatise of 1582, the second to the Ensign and Sergeant, and 'next unto them must be lodged the Drumme-plaiers and Fluite'. Here were drummers represented as a separate 'corps'—though that word was not applied to them until much later. They were certainly by then a cut above the privates who were paid eightpence a day compared with the drummers' 12d. They were already being chosen to make the dangerous parleying missions to the enemy 'to redeem and conduct prisoners and deliver messages which required knowledge of the enemy's tongue' as Sir Ralph Smythe wrote of them. This set them apart as the elite they were to remain, in addition to the prime element of their superiority, their mastery of the difficult technique of drum beating.

Some 40 years before Luis Gutserres de la Vega wrote *De re militari* in 1582, drummers had already established themselves as a distinctive and integral part of the army which Henry VIII was continually leading into battle against the French. On July 14, 1544 he landed an army of 30,000 men at Calais and intended

Drummer of Farrington's Regiment of Foot (W Y Carman)

making at once for Paris. But he decided he would first lay siege to Boulogne, and the march of this army down the coast was headed by a rousing posse of drummers and 'viffleurs'. It was not long before Governor Vervin surrendered the town to Henry whose drummer will doubtless have acted as go-between in the protracted negotiations.

The event which is regarded as consolidating drums and fifes as a fixture in British military music was the expedition ordered by Mary Tudor, Henry's daughter, in 1557. An English army of 10,000 under the Duke of Savoy landed in the Spanish Netherlands, joined forces with the army of Philip II of Spain, and crossed the frontier into

'The King's Shilling' by E Penny. Recruiting to the beat of the drum in 1770.

Lord George Lennox and The 25th Regiment in Minorca in 1771. Painting attributed to Giuseppe Chiesa.

Reproduced by courtesy of the National Army Museum.

James White, Bass Drummer, 1st Royal Cheshire Militia, 1805.

Reproduced by courtesy of the National Army Museum.

Drum Major and Pioneers, Grenadiers Company, 1815, after C Hamilton Smith.

France. Once again they were headed by drummers and fifers. In Picardy they besieged the fortress of St Quentin which held out for 14 days but finally surrendered on August 10 after 4,000 of the Scots and French defenders had been killed.

Drums and Fifes? The two would seem to be inseparable. Indeed for a time they were played by a one-man band. In Henry VIII's favourite ship the *Mary Rose* when it capsized off Spithead on July 19, 1545 were three three-holed 'tabor-pipes' and a small leather covered side-drum with its wooden stick. They were discovered in a store on the orlop deck when the ship was raised in 1982, and can to-day be seen in the Mary Rose Museum in Portsmouth Docks.

A tabor-pipe stuck in the mouth was played with the left hand, and a tabor/drum, its strap (carriage) slung over the shoulder, was beaten with a stick held in the right hand. The *Mary Rose* had a small band on board to entertain the Captain and his officers, and these were some of their instruments. They had no military significance. The 185 soldiers on board were there to board enemy ships which came alongside not to take part in any land operation.

But for the most part a drum and a fife had separate performers, one to beat, one to play and needing two hands for both.

The word 'fife' is the English phonetic pronunciation of the German-Swiss word 'pfeiff'. Both are an onomatopeia of the sound of air whistling through a hollow tube or pipe. It was what in a modified form (with keys) became a flute. A 'piper' can mean a man who plays a fife or a bagpipe. A bagpipe is a very early form of musical instrument and found in various forms all over the world. Though they

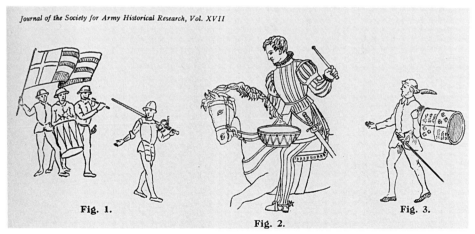

Journal of the Society for Army Historical Research, Vol. XVII

Fig. 1.

Fig. 2.

Fig. 3.

Drums at the Siege of Boulogne 1544.

played them many years before, there were no *official* bagpipers in a Scottish regiment, paid for out of the Public Purse, until 1854; and *all* Highland regiments did not get permission to have them till 1881. The concept of bagpipes and drums playing together as a military instrumental grouping did not come until around 1860.

Swiss mercenaries soldiering all over Europe began having drummers and fifers making music for their infantry in the fifteenth century. The idea was copied by certain English regiments who encountered them on the continent, but for some time no one could invent an English word for them. So in military circles they called the side-drum half of the combination a *sweche* (swiss) and the fifes *schweitzer pfeiffen*. As the provider of folk dance music in England, as seen, the combination was as old as the hills. Nudged by the example of the Swiss, its application to the infantry came easily. To the troops the fife added a lilt to the stark drum beat, but many thought its sound too ear-piercing. Shakespeare has one of his characters in *The Merchant of Venice* talk of the 'vile squeaking of the wry-necked fife'-the player marching in file had to turn his head to the left so that his pipe did not stick into the back of the man in front. A drummer did not have to read music but a fifer did. There were 'drummers' and 'fifers'. Some drummers could beat a drum and play a fife. Some fifers could play a fife and beat a drum. In the regimental establishments and records of the time the word is almost always 'Drummer'-more confusingly often 'Drumme'. But it must be taken to cover either a man who could only beat a drum, a man who could beat a drum and play a fife, or a man who could only play a fife. It was unlikely however that 'Fifer' would only refer to a drum beater; or 'Drum Beater' to a fifer. The Drum-Major taught the men how to beat a drum, the Fife-Major (of whom less is heard) how to read music and play a fife. Camp Calls were sometimes made on drums and fifes, sometimes on drums only. On the march, when the men were not singing unaccompanied (the most popular 'music' ?), they were helped on their way either by rhythms beaten by drums alone or by tunes played on fifes accompanied by drums, or by fifes alone. But the sound was almost always described as The Drums.

On important ceremonial occasions such as the Grand Proceeding from Westminster Hall to Westminster Abbey for the coronation of James II in 1685 drummers and fifers had a place of honour. A fifer walked immediately behind William Welles, the Dean's Beadle, who led the procession. He was dressed in a livery coat of scarlet cloth richly laced with gold and silver and lined with woollen shalloon. He wore blue breeches and a hat laced with gold and silver. On his back and chest he wore His Majesty's cipher and crown. Behind him came four side-drummers dressed in the same way. Their drums bore the royal arms and were draped with scarves of crimson taffeta fringed with silver. Each would have carried a sword of the same kind as the infantry. In his *Souldier's Accidence* of 1643 Francis Markham said the drummer 'is not bound to any armes at all more than his sword which in former times was not allowed but with the point broken' which would suggest he was a non-combatant which was not the case.

Behind the four side-drummers came the Drum-Major walking alone resplendent in a fine scarlet coat laced with gold and silver, and a crimson scarf of crimson taffeta about his waist fringed with gold.

Drum-majors had been around for a good hundred years, for as long at any rate as there had been men or boys who needed to be taught how to drum, but not always with that name. And there was a period when officially his role was considered superfluous between 1657 and 1680 – though unofficially that did not seem to make the slightest difference. He had become indispensable as the mentor of drummers and, with his magnificent staff the traditional symbol of colourful pomp and circumstance which earned him the contempt of the Puritans but pride of place in King James's procession.

The staff was more than just the most precious part of his insignia, a theatrical prop for tossing and twirling – copied from the Turks? It was strictly functional. Certain positions of holding it indicated certain instructions. The staff –'maces' are for lord mayors – made for the Drum-Major of The Honourable Artillery Company of London in 1671 has survived, and can be seen to-day at their headquarters. On parade he was the most lavishly dressed man in the regiment. Later on his lace alone was to cost £3 15s which was almost three times the value of his drum (£1 16s 6d).

He is not to be confused with the Bandmaster, the Director of Music and conductor of a military band of musicians, who had yet to come on the scene – and, when he did was not in uniform at all. Up to the 1860s the bandmaster was a civilian who wore 'civvies' and more often than not was a foreigner, though never of course a citizen of France, England's traditional enemy. It was not until 1803 that an Army Regulation authorised the use of a man from each company to be trained as a musician and a sergeant to be Sergeant of the Music. However one of the last acts of Charles II before he died in 1685 was to establish a regimental band of 12 hautboys (oboes), and ever since bass drummers of the Grenadier Guards Band have won dark blue armbands with a fleur de lys as a sign of mourning for their founder king.

The military manuals of the Stuarts took the drum-major for granted. Robert Ward devoted a whole chapter to his duties and office in *Animadversions of Warre* (1639). That he himself was expected to face the enemy as a messenger is made clear by Richard Elton in his *Compleat Body of the Art Military* of 1659. A drum-major, he said, must not only be proficient in the drummer's art but 'well skill'd in several languages and tongues'. From July 1655 the Lord Protector had a drum-major in each of the 13 infantry regiments which he organised for the field and garrison forces in Scotland. Up to 1690 the only regiments with a drum-major on their establishment however were the Foot Guards and the First Foot. A drum-major certainly took part in the military funeral of the Duke of Albemarle (General Monk) in 1670. By 1700 ever infantry regiment had a drum-major.

But they did not appoint the drummers. This was done by an officer in the royal household called The Drum-Major-General. In 1689 one John Mawgridge became Drum-Major-Generall of All His Majesty's Forces – the first. Within two years he had secured 144 drummers for six of the royal regiments. He charged a fee of six shillings a head, and earned £30 a year which was ten pounds less than the annual cost of his livery garb. He coupled the job with that of Drum-Major of the Royal Household. He was the drum-major in the coronation procession of James II and he was wearing the livery he had bought in 1674 at a cost of £52. Three of his family had served as drummers in the King's Music. The first 'King's Drum-Major' was William Gosson who had been a drummer since 1603. When he died in 1629 he was succeded by Robert Tedder.

A less glamorous duty was imposed on the drum-major when in 1680 it was decided to dispense with regimental provost-marshals. These were the officers who in camp and in the field headed the military police and were responsible for apprehending, locking up and punishing offenders of military law. Regimental Quartermasters took over their duties, but supervision and infliction of punishment ordered by a court martial devolved on the Regimental Drum-Major and his drummers. At a flogging the Provo handed out the rods and gave the first stoke; he organised all the other barbaric forms of punishment which the authorities had devised to maintain discipline. From 1680 his place in this regard was taken by the drum-major and the actual floggings were administered by drummers whose arms and wrists had grown strong by the constant beating of calf skin. Clifford Walton, who in 1894 wrote a history of the Standing Army from 1660 to 1700, saw it as the degradation of drummers to the office of regimental executioners. It soon became a confirmed custom which set The Drums even further apart from the rank and file, though this time not for their prowess as the admired parleyers and drum beaters but as the feared chastisers with whom it was important not to cross swords. For who knows but when it became your turn to be tied to the whipping post, your enemy Drummer Tomkins would make a point of laying in with particular ferocity. But if, on the other hand, the drum-major who stood beside the flagellator considered the beating was not for any reason (such as sympathy with the offender) being delivered as whole-heartedly as custom required, the drummer was himself in danger of finding himself on the halberd.

Drummers took no part in the Gatloup (Gantelope, Gauntlet) inflicted on the bare back of the culprit by his own comrades with willow wands as he ran between a line of them. But they beat as noisy flams and rolls as they could to drown the victim's cries. They and the drum-major were present however to set up the Wooden Horse. For this a soldier who had absented himself from the watch was sat for half an hour upon the sharp ridge of wooden boards which composed the back of the 'horse'. His hands were tied behind his back and his feet were loaded with muskets. His offence was written across his back, and the punishment was considered more humiliating than painful. It was a light offence. A life sentence was imposed for more serious misdemeanors. 'No souldier, either Horse or Foot, shall presume in marching to straggle from his Troop or Company, or to march out of his rank, upon pain of death.' And at the execution of a straggler the drummers would attend with muffled drums, and make sure the sentence was carried out with due solemnity. Not only floggers but undertakers.

How great a contrast to the hearty occasions when, in the words of a contemporary, the health of King Charles II was drunk at the head of every regiment with drums beating 'and so enthusiastic was their hilarity that, the toast having been duly honoured, they beat out the bottom of their drums'!

Leading the Grand Proceeding to Westminster Abbey for the coronation of James II 1685.

Except in such matters as keeping in line, there was a big divide between the man on Horse and the man on Foot. And of those mounted on horses in the British Army of the seventeenth century there were two groups, Dragoons and Cavalry. Dragoons were mounted infantry, musketeers on horseback. They derived their name from the French word *dragon*, decribed in 1625 as 'short piece with a barrel sixteen inches long of full musket bore fitted with a firelock'. They rode ahead to a bridge or a pass, dismounted and fought on foot. They lined hedges and ditches – 'outpost work'.

A dragoon wore no defensive armour. He did not carry a pistol, only a sword and a firelock musket which, unlike a matchlock, could be fired on horseback. Cromwell had one regiment of dragoons in the New Model Army, and they wore the red coats of the infantry, and hats not helmets. They were given inferior horses. A mount for a trooper in the Cavalry cost around ten pounds; a nag for a dragoon half that sum.

Each company of dragoons had two side-drummers, as in the infantry. A royal warrant of 1684 ordained that dragoons were Foot in garrison and Horse in the field. They were slowly becoming Cavalry proper, but they still manoeuvred to the beat of a drum. A dragoon drummer was the counterpart of a cavalry trumpeter. He beat upon a single, large, infantry pattern brass side-drum slung from his right shoulder and resting on his left thigh. He was not replaced by a trumpeter until 1765.

The Cavalry who fought on horseback beat drums on horseback. For this they found the infantry's side-drum unsuitable. They did not need a drum for signalling – they did that by trumpet – only on parade and for ceremonial. The drum they used was a larger version of the Arabian 'naker' which, as seen, had been adopted by European armies at the time of the Crusades but unlike the tabor had fallen into disuse. In England it re-emerged in the middle of the sixteenth century as the 'kettledrum' – through the English word was not coined until 1660. It resembled a big kettle or cauldron of the kind found in the galley of Henry VIII's *Mary Rose*. It was altogether more sizeable than the side-drum, and as the Turks had strung them over their shoulder in pairs, so the Europeans secured them one of either side of their horses.

The innovation of mounted kettle drummers in the train of the envoys whom King Ladislaus of Hungary sent to France in 1457 to treat for the hand of the Princess Madeleina, daughter of the French King Charles V, made a great impression, and far beyond Paris. They were still remembered nearly a hundred years later when England's Henry VIII, ever anxious to steal a march on his rivals, sent emissaries to Vienna, then the entreport of oriental trade, to purchase a pair of kettledrums which could be beaten on horseback 'after the Hungarian manner'. He also secured craftsmen who knew how to make and repair them, and experienced performers who knew how to beat them and teach Englishmen.

That was in 1542. At the Christmas festivities organised for Henry's son King Edward VI in 1551 there was music from 'a Kettel Drom with his boye' and a drummer and a fifer dressed in Turkish costume. Unlike the one-note side-drum, the pitch of a kettledrum could be adjusted (although probably not till later). Its body (or shell) was of copper or silver, and was similar to the *heerpauken* of the German army. When dismounted it was carried by a man on his back and beaten by another walking behind him. But it was hanging high in pairs on either side of a magnificent steed that kettledrums were displayed in full splendour.

When a Standing Army was established in England in 1660 kettledrums were reserved for the Life Guards. One John Barteeske was appointed His Majesty's Kettledrummer. A cavalcade headed by Life Guards with kettledrummer and trumpeters greeted the restored King Charles II in St George's Fields on May 29 1660. From then on kettledrums assumed an aura of majesty which was religio-magical. For a long time their use was confined to nobility and royalty. Permission for a regiment to have kettledrums was given only by the King or a high-ranking nobleman. In his *Pallas Armata* of 1683 Sir James Turner wrote:

There is another Martial Instrument used with the Cavalry which they call a Kettle-drum. There be two of them which hang upon the Horse before the Drummer's Saddle on both of which he beats. They are not ordinary. Princes, Dukes and Earls may have them with those Troops which ordinarily are called their Life-guards, so may Generals and Lieutenant Generals, though they be not Noble-men. The Germans, Danes and Sweeds permit none to have them under a Lord Baron unless they have taken them from an Enemy.

The Cavalry were not the only arm of His Majesty's Forces to have kettledrums. From 1689 the Master General of Ordnance (Artillery) had as part of his entourage a pair of kettledrums mounted on a chariot drawn by four white horses. The first mention of this extraordinary vehicle which accompanied the train of artillery in the Duke of Marlborough's campaigns in the next century was in a royal warrant of February 27, 1691. It required a train of brass ordnance to be in readiness for Flanders. It listed the officers who were to accompany it and their pay, and it ended with:

Kettle drummer	**4.0**
His coachman	**3.0**

Another warrant of two years later gave the name of the kettledrummer as John Burnett and the coachman as John Humphreys. Just what function they performed in the field is not clear – probably not to signal to the gunners but maybe by occasional beatings to encourage them in their noisy duties. The chariot and its precious burden could have been what The Colours were to an infantry regiment, a trophy which defied the enemy to capture it. Whatever its practical role it will certainly have given a sense of grandeur and majesty to the artillery command post and, so long as it stood firm and the drums went on beating, boosted morale.

There was a time, it seems, when the Artillery had side-drums and fifes. According to Francis Grose, at the siege of St Quentin in 1557 Henry VIII's

> **captain general had two trumpets, one drum and one fife; the lieutenant general one trumpet; the high mareschal one trumpet, one drum and one fife; the captain general of the infantry six wyfflers, one drum and one fife; and the master of ordnance one drum and one fife.**

But perhaps they were ousted by the kettledrums and their ostentatious chariot? Or kept on to make music when the guns were silent ? James II had made the Cavalry the senior arm when in every other European army the Infantry came first (and still does). So the Cavalry clung to their 'superior' kettledrums with their air of nobility, apart from being unable to find any use for any kind of instrument other than a trumpet. Drums and Fifes – 'The Drums' – were of the Infantry. They had been part of the establishment of the regular regiments of the line and the Guards since 1660. After 40 years however the fife gradually (and probably never entirely) lost favour. Though there was never an offical ban from on high, an unofficial anti-fife lobby managed to spread the idea that 'real' soldiers only marched to the manly beat of the unaccompanied side-drum which was the only true means of conveying camp and field calls. Adulterated by the squealing of a fife, the precise beat of the drum lost its edge, they felt.

A certain prejudice against the military fife had been expressed by Francis Markham in his *Five Decades* as early as 1622:

> **The Phiphe is but onely an Instrument of pleasure not of necessitie, and it is to the voice of the Drum and Souldier should wholly attend and not the aire of the whistle. For the one (which is the Drumme) speakes plainely and distinctly, the other speakes loud and shrill but yet curiously and confused.**

As a military music maker the fife also lost its popularity. And Dr Henry Farmer thought he knew why.

> **Probably the real reason for dropping the fife was the advent of the hoboy (oboe) into the Horse Grenadiers in 1678. The new instrument, borrowed from the French service, which had previously been influenced by Turkish bands of *zurnas,* had what Mozart called 'an impudence of tone' which stood out menacingly over all the other wood-wind instruments, even the 'squealing of the wry-necked fife' of Shakespeare. It soon came to be adopted by regiments of dragoons which, being treated as infantry, had side-drums. It then found its way into the foot guards and regiments of infantry, and completely ousted the fife from its old position.**

For whatever reason, the side-drum alone was the medium of signalling in the camp and in the field, and for regulating the marching on parade in British infantry regiments, for some 50 years between 1695 and 1745, though drums and fifes continued to hold their place in court military music. During that period 'The Drums' meant just that and nothing more.

EIGHTEENTH CENTURY

Chapter 3

BASS DRUMMER 7TH ROYAL FUSILIERS, 1790.

3   He Thinks He Turns The World Around

Heyday of the Drum-Major; Return of the Fife; With the Colours in the Square; Drum-beaters for the London Militia; Punishment and Funeral Duties; Drumming out; Red waistcoats, Black Drummers; Recruiting by Beat of Drum; Crying Down the Credits; All Debts Paid.

An off-duty drummer who had learnt to play the fife kept his hand in – and his lips – when away from the parade ground, the marching column and the fighting where it was now taboo, by playing tunes to his comrades which reminded them of the girls they had left behind them and made campaigning more bearable. He once had to be on call for delivering billets doux – 'for Honour or Ladies' loves he makes composition for single encounters provided it be on foot'. But now he created a romantic mood by playing a sentimental air or two on the fife, with drum accompaniment. Francis Markham, who censured the fife for its high-pitched tone, was nonetheless aware of the part it played in military life through giving pleasure with non-military music.

> When his duties in the Field are finished, if then being retired into the Tent he have the other artificiall and Musicall straines wherewith to steale away the minds and ears of his hearers, it will be a geat honour to him. Neither for mine owne part have I heard more sweet or more solemn melodie than that which the Drumme and Flute hath afforded.

Out of the tent, the drum took over as the most effective means of signalling for the infantry, though there were times, it seems, when by itself it was just not loud enough. 'Thare was orders for our drum-major to beet a parley' remembered the un-named Royal Dragoon in the Spanish Succession War describing the battle of Brihuega of 1710,

> **but it was not heard the first nor second time, but third time it was heard and the enemie stood before all the time & when the parly was heard they came to our breastwork & talk'd with us, for our Genlls had all the writings ready & the Duck of Vandome readily signed them.**

The champions of the drum however would countenance no criticism of its wonderful effects. Writing after the return of Drums *and* Fifes, Sir John Hawkins claimed it was ridiculous to hold that music was merely instrumental. The strokes of an anvil, he said, had a metrical ratio, and the most uniform monotony might be broken into various qualities. The drum, only capable of expressing the various measures and modifications of time, owed all its energy to what in poetry would be called Metre. That was nothing more than a regular and orderly co-mixture of long and short qualities.

> **Who can hear these uttered [by the drum], who can attend to that awful interchange of measures which is calculated to express, and that in a regular subjection to metrical laws, without feeling that he is acted upon like a mere machine ?**
> **With the utmost propriety therefore does our great dramatic poet style this instrument the Spirit-stirring drum; and with no less policy do those act who trust to its efficacy in the hour of battle, and use it as the means of exciting that passion which the most eloquent oration imaginable would fail to inspire.**
> *(A General History of the Science and Practice of Music)*

Inside Britain the no-fife lobby flourished under the influence of people whose pronounced views contrasted with the majority who were probably fairly indifferent. In any case 'the British Army' was comparatively small. In 1687 the army of James II was half the size of Cromwell's New Model Army; and a Standing Army was still illegal in Britain in peace time without the consent of Parliament in the reign of William and Mary. When he vacated the throne and fled to the continent in 1688 James had signed an instrument of disbandment of such regiments as existed, but Parliament halted it to meet the threat of a Jacobite rebellion in Ireland and war in Flanders. The army was not only not stood down – 11 new cavalry and 67 new infantry regiments were added between 1700 and 1800 – but Lieutenants in the counties were commissioned to raise volunteer units which would help the regular army repel invaders and keep public order.

Under an Act of 1662 the Lieutenant of the City of London was commissioned to levy trained bands and raise the 'auxiliaries' which became The London Militia. In 1715 the Court of Lieutenancy of London rated their drummers very highly and took measures to ensure they were not deprived of them.

Drummers to have protection.

Whereas by Law and the Ancient Custom of this City no Drummer belonging ot this City's Regiments ought to be Pressed and drawn out of this City's Service; therefore Ordered That the Colonels of the said Regiments respectively, do give Protection under their Hands and Seals to one Drummer in every Company of their said Regiments.
(*Court of Lieutenancy of London Minutes*, 4 October 1715)

When a regiment found itself aboard, the absence of fifes struck a jarring note. From 1714 the Kings of Great Britain had been German, the descendants of James I's daughter Elizabeth who had married the so-called Winter King of Bohemia. In 1749 James's great-great-grandson George II, Elector of Hanover, led an army of Hanoverian and Hessian troops against the French who, with King Frederick of Prussia, had attacked the forces of the Austrian Empress Maria Theresa, head of the House of Hapsburg. Frederick then declared war against England, and British and Hanoverian troops fought side by side throughout the War of the Austrian Succession.

The fife had never been abandoned in Germany, and the combined British-Hanoverian operation made the British regiments grow accustomed once more to the sound of the fife backing the beat of the drum, and gradually brought back into usage the Beat and Tune tradition of 50 years before.

The 26 year old Duke of Cumberland, younger son of George II, who was Commander-in-Chief of the British Army and leader of the allied forces in Flanders, ordered British Guards regiments to have drum beating accompanied by fifes when they were in camp in Maestricht in 1747. In that year the 19th Yorkshire Regiment, the Green Howards, became the first marching regiment to re-adopt fifes. When the war ended in the following year with the Peace of Aix-la-Chappelle, the Royal Artillery had fifers and a Fife Major who were taught by John Ulrich, a Hanoverian fifer brought over from Flanders by one Lieutenant Colonel Belford when the allied army broke up and returned to their respective countries.

It was no longer the fife of James II's coronation procession which were issued to these units but a simple, one-keyed flute capable of playing a much wider range of music, and gave an added lustre to routine Camp and Field Calls which, along with army organisation and the fighting of battles, became more sophisticated. In 1768 Thomas Simes summarised the Public Beatings of the Drum in Garrison in his *Military Course for the Government and Conduct of a Battalion* as:

Instruments of Military Musick 1786 (from Francis Grose
Military Antiquities)

To be at the General is an order for the whole to make ready to march; the Assemblee to repair to their colours; and the March commands them to move; the Reveille at daybreak warns the soldiers to rise and the centries [sic] to cease challenging; the Troop assembles them together to call over the roll and inspect the men for duty; the Retreat is beat at sunset for calling over the roll again to warn men for duty and read the orders of the day; the Taptoo beats at ten o'clock every night in summer and nine in winter; the soldiers must then repair to their quarters or barracks when the non-commissioned officers of each squad call over their rolls and every man must remain there till reveille next morning.

Twenty years later Francis Grose listed 15 different Beats of the Drum for the Infantry in his *Military Antiquities* in great detail. The General was beaten instead of Reveille only when the whole camp was to march. He made a clearer differentiation between Retreat and Taptoo. Retreat was beaten at sunset in garrison and at gun-firing in camp when pickets were formed – 'in fortified places it is a signal for the inhabitants to come in before the gates are shut'. Taptoo was the signal for soldiers to retire to their quarters or barracks and 'to the sutlers to draw no more liquor from whence it derives its name; the taptoo is seldom beat in camp.'

To Arms was a signal to summon soldiers to their alarm posts on some sudden occasion. The Church Call was for an obvious purpose, though less obvious is why it was also known as Beating The Bank. The Pioneers Call 'known by the appellation of Round Heads and Cuckolds', was for pioneers to come and dig; The Serjeants Call got sergeants running to the orderly room; The Drummers Call summoned drummers to the head of the colours or to the place where it was being beaten.

Field Calls still included The Preparative 'a signal to make ready for firing'; and The Chammade 'a signal to desire a parley with the enemy'.

There were also several other beats in different corps for particular signals, he said, such as The Long Roll for turning out the regiment in camp; and doubling The Troop to break from grand to sub-divisions.

In *The Military Medley*, which he wrote in 1768, Thomas Simes produced four plans showing how a battalion should form up, indicating the position to be taken by the Musick and by the Drummers and Fifers, establishing official recognition of the restoration of the latter in spite of the still universal use of the term 'beat' which presumably was purely a technical one for sounding a call by whatever means.

BATTALION IN FIRING ORDER

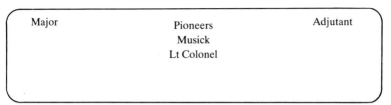

Major   Pioneers   Adjutant
                         Musick
                         Lt Colonel

Orderly   Drummers
        Colonel

BATTALION SIX DEEP IN SEMI-CIRCULAR ORDER
to oppose cavalry which may be useful at the Debarking of Troops or for Necessity, Making use of
either Wood, Water & c to secure the rear

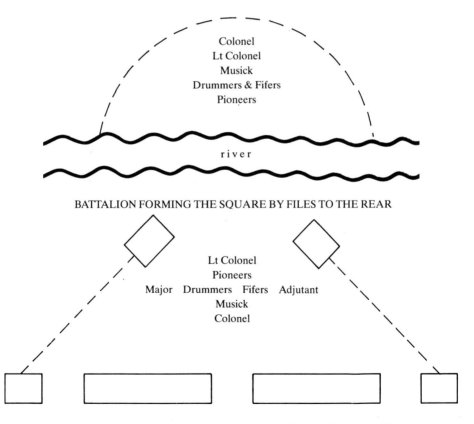

Colonel
Lt Colonel
Musick
Drummers & Fifers
Pioneers

r i v e r

BATTALION FORMING THE SQUARE BY FILES TO THE REAR

Lt Colonel
Pioneers
Major   Drummers   Fifers   Adjutant
Musick
Colonel

A fourth plan showed a Square formed with angles open, Musick in the centre with Drummers
and Fifers; and an Oblong Square formed by companies, the Grenadiers in the front and a Light
Infantry company at the rear, and Musick Drummers and Fifers in the middle.

The 46th Regiment, 1837 – watercolours by Michael Angelo Hayes. Reproduced by courtesy of the National Army Museum.

Drum Major, drummers, fifers and privates.

Attested and established Drummers and Fifers were not part of Musick, which was composed of musicians who had not been attested and were not strictly 'in' the Army. Simes's plans make plain their separate identities. Drummers and Fifers had existed long before the appearance of the embryo military band which the eighteenth century called Musick. They had independent functions, for which they came responsible in the previous century, and have remained an independent body ever since.

It is difficult to see what role the musicians could have played inside one of those squares, but their presence must have been greatly appreciated in the column of march. 'I'll answer for myself never to think any march too long' wrote Donkin in his *Military Collection* of 1777, 'providing a band accompanies the corps – nay how inspiring even is the drum and fife'.

Not that to-day's afficionados will forgive him that 'even'!

Thomas Simes had advice for his readers in 'the Choice of a Music Master, Drum and Fife Major'. The three men had their own functions but required the same qualities.

They should be men whose regularity, sobriety, good conduct and honesty can most strictly be depended upon; that are most remarkably clean and neat in their dress, that have an approved ear and taste for music and a good method of teaching without speaking harshly to the youth or hurrying them on too fast.

James Gillray cartoon – recruiting, 1809.

There was little demand as yet for military Music Masters but it was the hey-day of the Drum-Major. There was still someone called Drum-Major-General but he no longer appointed the side-drummers of infantry regiments and would appear in fact to have been deprived of every duty. Why it was thought necessary to retain the position is a mystery, and it savours of corruption. Apparently from 1689 to 1705 it was held by one man on behalf of another of the same name. The dummy Drum-Major-General who played that trick reaped his reward however when in 1706 he was murdered.

John Clothier, who had been a side-drummer under John Mawgridge and was the son of a drummer in the royal household, was appointed Drum-Major-General in 1719. John Conquest, who doubled the job with that of Drum-Major of the Royal Household, held the post from 1755 to 1769. In 1777 George III appointed 'our trusty and well-beloved Charles Stuart, gent' Drum-Major-General of his forces; and when he died, according to the *London Gazette* of March 5 1791, 'Drum Major William Hood of the Coldstream Regiment of Foot Guards is to be drum-major-general vice Charles Stuart deceased.' He was the last.

The office was in line with the 'useless, expensive and unnecessary offices' condemned by Edmund Burke in his Regulations in the Receipt of His Majesty's Exchequer Act of 1783, part of his overall Plan for Economic Reform, sinecures such as Tally Cutter and Usher of the Exchequer. It was Horace Walpole's surrender of the latter patent which led to the creation of His Majesty's Stationery Office in 1786. The useless and unnecessary post of Drum-Major-General was probably swept away in the same drive for economy and efficiency, particularly in the unproductive royal household, which was largely prompted by the Government's need to pay for continuing the war against His Majesty's rebellious subjects in British North America.

As the role of the Drum-Major-General diminished to the point of vacuity, that of the Regimental Drum-Major increased – though unofficially. According to Francis Grose *(Military Antiquities* 1786) 'the regimental drum-majors have no extra pay from government, but receive some addition by stoppage from the pay of the young drummers and contributions from the captains.' A drum-major appeared on the establishment of The Buffs in 1702 and was paid 1s 6d a day, the first time a drum-major had a recognised position in the regiment.

In 1777 the author of *The Rudiments of War* was claiming that every regiment had a drum-major though only the Foot Guards and Royal Artillery were allowed one 'officially', that is paid for out of the Public Purse. A drum-major was put on the establishment of the Cadet Company Royal Artillery in 1744. The first to hold the office was John Hollingshead, appointed while the regiment was in Flanders. But three years later he was called home

Woolwich, 16 June 1747

To Colonel Bedford.

All our Drummers being at present boys, and three of them
lately Enterred [enlisted], the General desires that you will
order the Drum-Major to England as we have nobody here
who can instruct them to beat.

In 1748 they got a Fife-Major too. On June 13 1753 he was on parade with the
Drum-Major, ten drummers and five fifers heading the Artillery in an army review
by King George II in Green Park. The drummers wore scarlet with blue facings
– it must have been a great sight.

See drummers with the fifers come,
And Carter with the massive drum;
The grand drum-major first doth stalk
With gold-knobbed stick and pompous walk,
And as he marches o'er the ground
He thinks he turns the world around.

The volunteer services were moving in the same direction – with help from the
Artillery. Wishing to increase the number of drummers in the London Militia 'in
case any Public disturbance should make it necessary to raise the several regiments',
in 1741 the Commission for the Lieutenancy of the City of London recommended
the appointment of 'a proper Person to do the office of a Drum-Major in training
up and instructing a sufficient number of Persons to supply each company with
one drummer.'

They found on enquiry that such training and instructing of drum beaters
could not be affected without the expense of much time and trouble. Three
guineas and upwards was usually paid for such instruction. However John Hyde,
one of the drummers of the Artillery Company, had offered to perform the service
for two guineas for each person he taught and qualified to act as a drummer in
the Militia Service. Hyde would receive the money after his pupil had enlisted as
a drummer in a City Militia company. They had no reason to expect that any
other qualified person would do this service for less. Their enquiries had shown
that apart from those who belonged to the King's Guards, the London Militia had
only 20 drummers of its own. However 24 drummers were thought necessary,
and had usually been employed in the Muster Marches of every regiment, that
was to say three drummers to every company. It was now going to be necessary
to have 24 drummers for the regiment on duty and another 24 for the relieving
regiment which would take over next day. So altogether they would need 48
drummers. They suggested the best way of supplying that number was to oblige the

commander of every company to have one drummer enlisted in his company as soon as possible,

> **and that the Drummer so enlisted be not one of those belonging to His Majesty's Guards because their Duty in the Guards would render it impracticable for them to be employed in the Trained Bands in Case of Publick Disturbance.**

At that same meeting of 16 July 1741, the Court of Lieutenancy ordered

> **That such Drum-beaters as are or shall be Listed in the several companys of the Militia of this City do for the future take the oaths appointed to be taken instead of the Oaths of Supremacy and Allegiance.**

A fortnight later John Hyde was duly appointed Drum-Major of the London Militia, and by October had been reported to have instructed 11 persons in the Art of Drum-Beating and that they had all been enlisted as drum-beaters in one of the companies. Whereupon he was paid Three and Twenty Pounds and Two Shillings.

A drummer of 1780.

Though most Foot Regiments in Britain had a drum-major after 1705, it took time for the practice to filter through to regiments overseas. No regiment is recorded as having one in the West Indies between 1704 and 1707. But before the death of Queen Anne in 1714 drum-majors were appearing in regiments outside Britain, though not mainly for the purpose of training new drum-beaters but to take over responsibility for carrying out the sentences of corporal punishment imposed by courts-martial.

A hundred years after the withdrawal of regimental provost-marshals the performance of his debasing duty had hardened into an accepted custom. In 1778 Thomas Simes was writing:

> **You are always to have with you your apparatus for punishing, as it is often found necessary to hold regimental court-martials at the drum-head, and it should be an established rule that a man that receives 100 lashes or more should pay you 2d, and if punished a second time for another offence, 6d. No cat to have more than nine tails.**

A later *Regimental Companion* enjoined the drum-major to see the cat-o-nine-tails properly prepared and to be careful that no extraordinary ingenuity was exercised to make knots 'heavier or more searching than the human frame could bear.'

> **God forbid that a prevalent report should be true relative to the insertion of lead in some cats that were used during the Irish effervescence! Left-handed drummers ought to be excused from being the means of adding unnecessary torture by cutting the back of the soldier across the former stripes which must be the case when right and left-handed drummers inflict the lashes.**

The author of *Cautions and Advices to Officers of the Army, particularly subalterns*, published in Edinburgh in 1777, however, warned his readers against 'Running the gauntlet in which if the criminal has a good share of heels and a little cunning he may not feel 20 lashes from the whole battalion'. There was no escaping the lashes when tied to the halberds of four sergeants in the centre of the whole regiment drawn up in a hollow square. Sentences ranged from 25 to 1,200 lashes but the average was between 300 and 700. These were given by the regimental drummers, 25 lashes at a time to the tap of a drum beaten in slow time. Supervising the whole punishment at close quarters were the drum-major, the sergeant-major and the adjutant.

It was known for drummer *boys* to be ordered to carry out the flogging to add to the humiliation, especially before a drumming out. Up to the middle of the nineteenth century a soldier discharged with ignominy was drummed out of the regiment with elaborate ceremony. The whole regiment formed up in two ranks facing inwards, with one end touching the barrack gate. At the other end the adjutant read out the offence and sentence to the culprit standing between his escort. The Provo Sergeant then cut off the soldier's badges, tore away his shoulder straps and buttons. Whereupon prisoner and escort marched down the ranks while the regimental drummers and fifers played The Rogues March. On his way down the prisoner had his sentence read over to him at regular intervals. The climax was his ejection from the barrack gates, followed by his possessions, and a kick to the backside administered by the smallest drummer of them all. Turning an unwelcome guest out of doors became known in civvy street as 'John Drum's Entertainment' as a result.

Equally sombre but less savage was the role of the regimental drummer at a funeral, his drums muffled, beating with the fifers The Dead March, an army ritual of long standing. 'When any dies' wrote Francis Markham,

the Drumme with a sad solemnitie must bring him to his grave. For it is the only mourner for the lost and the greatest honour of Funerals. Whence it comes that any man dying (above the degree of common soldier), the Drummer performing the last duty, may for his fee challenge the sword of the deceased.

How great a contrast to doleful ceremonial such as this was the part played by the military drum in the triumphal celebration of victory!

In July 1758 Louisburg fell. The whole island of Cape Breton was reduced. The fleet to which the court of Versailles had confided the defence of French America was destroyed. The captured standards were borne in triumph from Kensington Palace to the City and were suspended in St Paul's Church amidst the roar of guns and kettledrums, and the shouts of an immense multitude. (Thomas B Macaulay, *Essay on W M Thackeray's History of the Earl of Chatham)*

The drummers contribution to public jubilation was not only the intoxicating sound of their beating but the brilliance of their uniforms. George II ordered an enquiry to be made into the State of the Army after the death of the Duke of Marlborough, and the House of Commons Committee reported in 1746. As a result, in 1751 a royal warrant was issued authorising new regulations regarding clothing.

Drummers' Cloathing

The Drummers of all the Royal Regiments are allow'd to wear the Royal Livery, Viz. Red, lined, faced and lapelled on the Breast with Blue and Laced with a Royal Lace; the Drummers of all other Regiments are to be cloathed with the colour of the Faceing of their Regiments lined, faced and lapelled on the Breast with Red and laced in such manner as the Colonel shall think fit for distinction sake, the Lace however being of the Colours of that on the Soldiers' Coats.

The front of drums were to be painted with the colour of the facing of the regiment, with the King's cypher and crown, and the number of the regiment under it.

In 1768 George III issued a similar warrant but it specified that the coats of drummers and fifers of Royal Regiments which were laced with red were to be white faced, lappelled and lined with red. They would wear red waistcoats and breeches. Other, non-royal regiments' drummers were to have the facing of their regiment faced and lapelled with red. Drummers and fifers were to wear black bear-skin caps, on the front of which was the King's crest in silver-plated metal on a black ground. The drums themselves were to be of wood. All drummers were to have a short sword with a scimitar blade. This sword was two and a half feet long and had a curved handguard, and was regulation dress until 1857. Only slight changes were made to drummers uniforms after 1768. In 1792 they were given brighter braid and epaulets. Lapels disappeared, but the cost remained a 'coatee' for a long time – short tails behind and short in front.

A trial costing of drummer's uniform made in 1764 by Andrew Regnier & Son, regimental tailors, shows that at £5 17s 5d it was more expensive than a sergeant's at £5 6s 0d, and very much more costly than a corporal's at £4 2s 9½d and a trumpeter's at £3 0s 3d. Regniers proposed charging £1 15s 0d for making a drummer's regimental suit, the main material being one and three quarter yards of blue cloth at 7s, which came to 12s 3d. And then there was nine yards of white and red 'Padua' at 1s 8d, and an unbelievable 54 yards of narrow worsted lace which luckily only cost threepence halfpenny a yard. The trial costing was not accepted and the broken down costing given by Thomas Simes in *The Military Medley* of 1768 shows they got the price down to under £4.

for Drummers

Cloathing, Hat and Lace	2s 6d
Cap, Grenadiers	14s
Sword & solid scabbard	8s
Shoulder belt	5s
Drum & case	£1 6s 6d
Drum sticks	2s
Shirts	2s
Roller or stock	6d
White gaiters	2s 3d
Black linnen ditto	1s 7d
Black tops	7d
Linnen drawers	2s 2d
Pair of shoes	4s 8d
Pair of stockings	2s
Knapsack and sling	2s 6d
Haversac	1s
Stock-buckle or clasp	5d
Garter ditto	4d
Leather garters	4d
Cocade	6d
Redcap and lining	5d

Simes reckoned that lace for a drum-major's uniform would alone cost £3 15s. But resplendent though a British drum-major could look on parade, his position as the most colourfully attired figure of the regiment was serioulsy challenged after the Sultan of Turkey in 1730 gave an entire Turkish military band in full costume to King Augustus II of Poland. It included a wide variety of percussion instruments never seen or heard in England – little marching kettledrums, triangles and cymbals, a big bass drum.

News of the Grand Porte's present, and of the remarkable sound it made, swept through Europe. Regiments vied with each other to be the first to incorporate at least one of these new instruments in their Musick. If they could not import a real, dark-skinned Eastern Mediterranean citizen of the Ottoman Empire to play it, the next best thing was to hire a coloured man from another part of the world. Any West Indian or African procured for this purpose would of course be the responsibility of the officers. They were musicians and not drummers, and extra to establishment.

Some British mounted regiments had anticipated the fashion. The 4th Dragoons are said to have had six drummers, some of whom were Moors, in 1715. Sir Robert Rich's Regiment of Dragoons (later The 4th Hussars) had a black drummer called Toby Gill in 1750 whose existence is known from his having killed a poor countrywoman in Suffolk. 'A very drunken and profilgate fellow', he was caught and hanged.

But the man who brought a spate of black drummer appointments in the British army was a naval man, Admiral Boscawen. Being in the Caribbean at the surrender of Guadeloupe in 1759, he cornered ten West Indian boys and brought them home in his ship. Once in England he presented them to his soldier brother who commanded Thomas Farrington's Regiment, the 29th Foot (late The 1st Battalion Worcestershire Regiment). Permission was obtained from King George III to retain them as drummers (percussion players), and the tradition of this regiment having black drummers persisted for 84 years, the last of the line dying in July 1843.

From then on it became The Thing to have black drummers in British military bands and dress them more and more fancifully. In the next century one of those in the band of the 29th Foot was to cause a sensation by wearing a muslin turban with a silver crescent in front surmounted by a scarlet hackle feather a foot high. He wore a silver-plated stock round his neck, a yellow cloth jacket à la hussar, the collar and cuffs of which were trimmed with black fur. His chest was embroidered with black silk cord and three rows of silver buttons. Underneath this he had a white waistcoat embroidered with crimson cord and silver buttons. Round his waist was a yellow and crimson sash, and at his side a Turkish scimitar. On his legs were scarlet pantaloons with a silver stripe and yellow Hessian boots. He was not just a musician but a mascot. Like his upkeep, his raiment was paid for by the officers who challenged all other regiments to produce a more exotically attired blackamoor to march at the head of The Musick or The Drums.

No regimental drum-major could compete with *that* sort of fancy dress.

Regiments took up the challenge not only to outshine in magnificence but in numbers. The more clashing and banging of big bass drums, triangles, tambourines, cymbals and marching kettledrums, the more they drowned the melody, and it became necessary to have more musicians who were playing the tune. Some regiments had as many as 16 percussionist/drummers. The 7th Royal Fusiliers commanded by the Duke of Kent had all its drummers negroes. The bass drummer was a very imposing fellow. He wore a headress of white cloth with a red feather on one side and a tassel on the other which always drew ripples of laughter from onlookers who thought it resembled a wedding cake. In his ears he had strings of cowrie shells which shook and rattled every time he beat the drum. His white coat and waistcoat had blue facings elaborately trimmed with red and yellow lace. Hanging from his waist was a buff apron, on his feet were white gaiters.

On one occasion at least the presence of black drummers in a British regiment abroad served a purpose unconnected with either percussion or attire. The Drum-major of the 88th Foot (Connaught Rangers) in Spain at the beginning of the Peninsular War was teenager Nicholas Thorp, son of a wealthy Lancashire merchant, who had run away from home and was a talented musician. In Campo Mayor, where the regiment was stationed, Nicholas fell in love with Jacintha Cherito daughter of the influential Sēnor Jose Alfonso Cherito the town's chief magistrate, who had more aristocratic plans for his daughter's marriage.

On the morning the 88th were due to move to another town, Jacintha was missing. Her father insisted that the CO search the regiment's baggage in which he was certain Jacintha was hiding disguised as a British soldier. The colonel agreed, but the girl was nowhere to be found in any of the many wagons and carts. So the band struck up and marched off with Nicholas at the head of them, and behind him a line of black drummers and cymbalists. On arrival at Monte Forte the regimental drum-major was seen running off with one of the 'negroes' to the nearest padre to get married. It was Jacintha of course, who had deceived her father by blacking her face and, with their connivance, dressing as one of the black drummers.

Drum-major Thorp was promoted Regimental Sergeant-major in the field when the RSM was killed at the Battle of Busaco, but four years later he was himself killed at the Battle of Toulouse fought 'by mistake' after Napoleon, unknown to Wellington, had already abdicated and the war was over.

Poster for German production of
The Recruiting Officer.

A colourful military uniform, and the thought that one day he might impress his girl by wearing one, played an important part in persuading youths who, unlike Nicholas Thorp, needed nudging to enlist.

Pryse Lockhart Gordon resisted the appeal of the Recruiting Sergeant who came to his village of Cullen in Invernesshire that day in the summer of 1770 when he was a boy of eight, but it was an occasion he never forgot.

He was a stout strapping fellow, carried his nose up in the air and strutted like our turkey-cock; his laced hat being adorned with large bunches of streaming ribbons, and a soldier behind him carrying fine colours with the king's arms on them, while the boy that beat the drum was not many inches taller than myself... The sergeant stood at the cross, and after a terrible rolling of the drum, made a speech in a sort of language which I did not readily understand but it was meant to be English. He promised all the brave fellows who would follow him great riches, and that he would show them a country where guineas were as rife as gooseberries, which he called groserts.

So he escaped the treatment which the young John Shipp received after he had failed to discount the recruiting sergeant's sales talk and handed himself over to his far from tender mercies.

On the following morning I was taken to a barber's and deprived of my curly brown locks... I was then paraded to the tailor's shop and deprived of my new clothes ... I was exceedingly tall for a boy of ten years age but notwithstanding this my clothes [red jacket, waistcoat, pantaloons and foraging cap] were much large ... My pride was humbled, my spirits dropped and I followed the drum-major hanging my head like a felon going to the place of execution.

'By beat of drum' was still the normal way of recruiting.

RECRUITING ORDER AND NOTICE OF BOUNTY 1725

These are to authorise you by Beat of Drum or otherwise to raise Volunteers in any county or part of this our Kingdom of Great Britain for a Regiment of Foot under your command for Our Service, to consist of Ten Companies of Two Sergeants, Two Corporals, One Drummer, and Forty Private Soldiers including the Widows' Men in each company.

The crowd round the market cross asked few questions. The attractive uniform, the beat of the drums and the urging of their fellow villagers were relied upon to overcome any personal distaste for campaigning. But for Scotsmen who could read, this printed Recruiting Order in 1782 posted on the walls did its best to play on their credulity and hide the true nature of army life.

HIS MAJESTY'S FIRST ROYAL REGIMENT
OF FOOT GUARDS

The greatest opportunity ever known for YOUNG SCOTCHMEN to raise themselves and Families.

Your Duty is a constant Pleasure, being only to attend and Guard his Majesty's Person at the Palace, and to the Theatres, Opera-houses, Masquerades and Reviews of different Regiments.

Under no restraint off duty, no roll-calling, dress as you please, follow any profession. Pay is 10d a day and 4s Subsistence a week & 15s a year Queen's Bounty, a Room to

yourself and 5 pints of choice Beer or good Cyder every day. So great an Opportunity as this cannot be supposed to last long; therefore, before it is too late, let all handsome young Men whose Hearts beat at the Sound of the Drum, and are above mean Employments, inquire after the Party commanded by Captain Dick.

The bounty was three guineas and a Crown. Anyone who brought in a good recruit received a guinea (£1 1s). Those who fell for such a yarn or allowed their emotions to get the better of them by yielding to stirring drum beats, were soon to find, like John Shipp, their spirits drooping—and worse to come.

The mother of the would-be soldier in Isaac Bickerstaff's pointed ballad-opera *The Recruiting Sergeant*, staged at the end of the eighteenth century, was under no illusion as to the detrimental effect which the sergeant's appeal would have on her son should he be weak enough to respond to it. At him she shouted:

> *Out upon thee, wicked locust !*
> *Worse in country than a plague !*
> *Men by thee are hocus-pocust*
> *Into danger and fatigue.*
>
> *   *   *   *   *
>
> *Then get thee a-trudging quick,*
> *For 'gad ! if I take a stick,*
> *I'll make thee repent*
> *When here thee were sent*
> *A-drumming for recruits.*

Unabashed, the recruiting sergeant soldiered on with the conventional glowing account of the excitement and romance of battle.

> *What a charming thing's a battle !*
> *Trumpets sounding, drums a-beating;*
> *Crack, crick, crack the cannons rattle;*
> *Every heart with joy elating.*
> *With what pleasure are we spying,*
> *From the front and from the rear,*
> *Round us in the smoky air,*
> *Heads and limbs and bullets flying !*
> *Then the groans of soldiers dying*
> *Just like sparrows, as it were.*

'Call you this charming?' cries the mother, 'It is the work of hell.'

Drumming round the market cross might tell the townspeople that the Army was requiring their attention, not to help them find recruits but to remind them of the average soldier's impecuniosity. Aware of a soldier's low pay, the Army saw to it that when a regiment arrived in a new town, the shopkeepers and tradesmen were warned about giving credit—or too much credit—to mostly illiterate Other Ranks, here to-day and gone tomorrow, and allowing them to run up debts they had not the slightest chance or intention of repaying. These were the days before soldiers were housed in barracks and were left to their own devices in the taverns and private houses in which they were billetted. That first day the Provost Sergeant would march to the market cross accompanied by drummers and fifers who then started 'beating' to attract attention. To the crowd who assembled the Provost Sergeant announced that anyone giving credit to members of the regiment which had arrived did so at their own risk.

This was known as 'Crying Down The Credits'. Before the regiment was about to leave the Provost Sergeant and the drummers would return to the centre of the town to tell shopkeepers that they were about to move and that it would be in their interests to stop giving further credit immediately. The likelihood of a hard-up, poorly paid soldier who had left the town for good ever returning to pay his debts were negligible. This ceremony was known as 'All Debts Paid'.

BASS DRUM AND CYMBALS, LINE REGIMENT, **1815.**

Chapter 4

KETTLE DRUMMER 1ST HORSE
1751
(NOW 4TH ROYAL IRISH DRAGOON GUARDS)

DRUMMER OF LIGHT DRAGOONS, 1766.

4 See The Conquering Hero Comes

Handel borrows kettledrums for oratorios, regiments capture French kettledrums as trophies; Blenheim and Dettingen; Drumming gives the game away at St Cas; Minden Day ritual; Artillery kettledrums in Flanders; the Cult of the Little Drummer Boy; John Shipp and Joseph Brome; Ballot System goes.

A Foot regiment left a town with The Drums and The Musick (its hautboys now augmented by horns, bassoons, trombones and clarionets) playing the Foot-March—or if they were Grenadiers the Grenadiers March. According to Francis Grose there was a time when they beat the Long March 'on the beating of which the men clubbed their firelocks and claimed and used the liberty of talking all kind of ribaldry respecting their amours and those of their officers', but presumably that was at a stop en route. 'This has for some time been very properly abolished' commented Grose in 1786.

Though plenty of marching music had been written such as those in Elizabeth Rogers's Virginall Booke of 1656, distinctive march music for each regiment only became the fashion very gradually, and indeed was not officially recognised until 1882. However, when the custom was encouraged by royalty, the trend, though unofficial, was hard to stop. Princess Augusta, daughter of George III composed a regimental march with an impressive drum solo in the middle called *The Royal Windsor* which was adopted by The Worcestershire Regiment. Queen Victoria's German mother, the Duchess of Kent, composed a regimental march for The Royal Horse Guards which was named after her. But on roads which would allow anything resembling 'marching'—and they were few and far between in Britain—it was the beating of the side-drum which gave the column cohesion.

A Horse regiment on the move had no need of drums to regulate their progress. Their kettledrums had a very different, more exalted role.

As seen, from their first appearance in Britain they were surrounded by an almost mystical aura which gave them an aloofness accentuated by being mounted haughtily in pairs astride powerful horses. High and mighty, draped with fringed banners, they could not fail to impress even when silent. Beating them forcibly with two padded sticks produced a thundering sound akin to the galloping of unbridled horses or an uncontrollable landslide. 'A drum, a drum, Macbeth doth come !' cried the witches in dread of what so unearthly a sound portended. It must have come from kettledrums. No wonder Frederick Handel chose kettlerums for the rolls he wrote into *Judas Maccabeus* composed in 1746 to celebrate the Duke of Cumberland's no-holds-barred victory over the Highlanders at Culloden. They could convey the terror of that terrible engagement as nothing else.

> *See the conquering hero comes !*
> *Sound the trumpets, beat the drums !*

Each of the four troops of Horse Guards, the staff of HM Royal Regiment of Horse, HM Own Regiment of Horse and two other regiments of Horse were allowed a kettledrummer in December 1735. The (horse) Grenadier Guards and the eight regiments of Dragoons however had neither kettledrums nor trumpets but hautboys and side-drummers. The Dragoon Guards, who had been so styled in 1746, and the Dragoons used side-drums until the Order of July 23, 1766 told them to exchange their drummers for trumpeters.

It is easy to imagine the role of these heavy brass or copper instruments measuring some 20 inches in diameter on great ceremonial parades and triumphal processions, but did they really take them into *battle* ?

From the number which were captured by either side in the continental wars of the eighteenth century, it would seem they did. 'Meanwhile the Duke of Marlborough ordered all his troops to enter the lines' wrote Tobias Smollet of the peak operation of 1704.

In this action the confederates took the Marquis d'Alegre and the Count de Horne, lieutenant-generals, one major-general two brigadier-generals, with many other officers and a great number of common soldiers; a large heap of standards, four colours, one pair of kettledrums and ten pieces of cannon.

This was the Battle of Blenheim. The Duke ordered that the captured kettledrums were to be carried at the head of the Royal Dragoons of Ireland. Some 96 yards of gold lace and three yards of blue velvet were bought for their adornment.

*'The Guard Room, Horse Guards' 1851
by F R Pickersgill. Reproduced by
courtesy of the National Army Museum.*

Drummer of The 1st Battalion The Connaught Rangers, 1898, specially drawn for The Royal Tournament 1988 by Peter Walton.

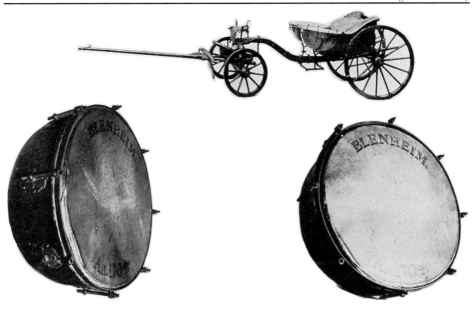

Drum-Major's Chariot and the Tower Drums.

They are said to have been carried at the heads of British regiments at the battles of Ramillies, Oudenarde and Malplaquet.

Four years after Blenheim the Duke of Marlborough had as head of the Hanoverian Cavalry the son of King George I, the young Electoral Prince of Hanover. On seeking permission to charge the French, the prince was told by his commander-in-chief he could do nothing of the sort. When, disregarding this order to stay put, the hot-headed young man at once led his men against the enemy, the Duke had him tried by court-martial which, the prisoner admitting the offence, degraded him from Major-General to Corporal. But only temporarily. Thirty years later, the royal corporal, restored to more exalted rank, and the reigning monarch, King George II, with equal impetuosity was leading troops against the French—on foot. The time was June 27, 1743 and the place near Dettingen on the river Main. It was the first battle of the War of the Austrian Succession.

The king exposed his person to a severe fire of cannon (wrote Smollett) **as well as musketry; he rode between the first and second lines with his sword drawn, and encouraged the troops to fight for the honour of England.**

When his horse bolted he marched with the first line of infantry. It was the last time a British King was to lead his army into battle in person.

The Battle of Dettingen ended in victory for the allied army which included the Kings Own Regiment of Horse and the Kings Own Regiment of Dragoons, later respectively The King's Dragoon Guards (now The 1st The Queen's Dragoons Guards) and the 3rd Hussars (now The Queen's Own Hussars), who lost three quarters of their strength. There had been great slaughter on both sides.

The Earl of Stair sent a trumpeter to Mareschal de Noailles, recommending to his protection the sick and wounded that were left on the field of battle; and these the French general treated with great care and tenderness. Such generosity softens the rigours of war, and does honour to humanity.

At some point in the battle a pair of silver kettledrums were captured from the French by a trumpeter either of the 7th Dragoon Guards or the 3rd Hussars—or were they one and the same? In 1876 a bandmaster of the 7th Dragoon Guards told George Potter & Co, the Aldershot drum makers, that the 3rd Hussars did in fact have a pair of silver kettledrums but they had captured them in Ireland. In 1985 Major Bulkeley, Second-in-Command of the Queen's Own Hussars, said four pairs of kettledrums had been captured from the French during the battle of 1743—the other three by non-British regiments in the allied army? He insisted however that the regiment of which The Queen's Own Hussars were the successors captured one of the pairs. Perhaps the trumpeter who by tradition laid hands on them acted on information brought back to him by a fellow trumpeter who had kept his eyes open, as required by the rule book, while on parley duty?

The English regiment had their own kettledrummers to beat the valuable trophies, and 29 years after the battle, on Lord Southampton being appointed Colonel of the Regiment, his wife marked the occasion by presenting the regiment with a solid silver collar, some three and a quarter inches high, to be worn by the man who beat the French 'Dettingen Drums'—probably a coloured man and one possessing an unusually long neck. It was hinged and fastened at the back like a clerical collar.

When in 1766 however the regiment's kettledrummers were exchanged for trumpeters, they had no one to play the French pair. So in 1778 the new Colonel of the Regiment, Lieutenant General Charles Fitzroy, asked Viscount Barrington, Secretary of State for War, for permission to add a kettledrummer and another horse to their establishment to play the trophy (which of course was not taken away from them). Permission was granted—and was indeed formally confirmed in 1959.

When they were not in use, the pair of French kettledrums were put in the Tower of London for safe keeping, but were destroyed in a fire that badly damaged the fortress in 1855. The following year they had replicas made by the London firm of Distin, which could be tuned in seven keys by turning a single screw. These replica silver kettledrums are still in the proud possession of The Queen's Own

Hussars, and so is Lady Southampton's 216 year old silver collar, which was not kept in the Tower, and is still worn by their kettledrummer.

The Queen's Own Hussars' silver kettledrums bear the regiment's battle honours in three groups, up to and including the South African War, the Great War and World War II. Having battle honours on the drums themselves is unique. They are the only drums of regiments of the Household Cavalry and Cavalry of the Line where the honours are not carried on drum banners and where the drums are carried uncovered. Up to the presentation of the Guidon to The Queen's Own Hussars in 1959, the silver drums were accorded the compliments of Regimental Colours.

Precisely how the Dettingen Drums came to be captured (by a trumpeter?) has never been recorded, but for it to have happened the French must have brought them on to the field of battle and had a specific use for them, as presumably the 3rd Hussars had for theirs. Rousing rolls broadcast at the right moment would have encouraged hard-pressed fighters to make the extra effort that would give them victory. Made at the wrong moment, drum-beating intended to raise morale could be disastrous.

After English troops under General Bligh had been landed on the beach of St Lunaire one September afternoon in 1758 to go and harry the French, the 'invasion fleet' moved down the coast to the Bay of St Cas. When the peasants began firing at his men from the hedges, General Bligh thought he should parley with them. He sent a priest, not a drummer, to tell them if they did not desist he would burn them out of hearth and home. Bligh set up camp that night three miles inland from the Bay of St Cas, so that next morning they could all re-embark on the ships in the bay and sail back to England. But overnight the French dug a trench round the bay to prevent the English marauders doing any such thing. Bligh considered he had no alternative but to reach the ships as best he may. Smollett thought this savoured of 'blind security and rash presumption'.

Had the troops decamped in the night without noise, in all probability they would have arrived at the beach before the French had received the least intelligence of their motion; and, in that case, the whole army consisting of about six thousand men, might have re-embarked without the least interruption. But instead of this cautious manner of proceeding, the drums were beaten at two o'clock in the morning, as if to give notice of intention to the enemy, who forthwith repeated the same signal.

Presumably in mock thanks for having given the game away.

They were on their way towards the bay before 3 am, but because of numerous halts and interruptions they did not reach it until nine to find the transports lying too far from the shore to let them embark. The French, all set to receive them, fired on them with their cannon. A good number of the English managed to clamber aboard the ships but a rearguard of 1,500 turned and charged the greatly superior enemy, panicked, faltered and broke. 'They fled in the utmost confusion pursued by the French who fell in among them with their bayonets fixed and made a great carnage.'

The mistake made the next year at the Battle of Minden had a happier ending. A mistimed advance by six British and four Hanoverian regiments against a greatly superior French force was redeemed by a show of copybook discipline and unsurpassed bravery. Unsupported, they marched through a cross-fire of cannon. On being ferociously charged by French cavalry, they held their ground until the horses were within 20 yards of them, and then fired volleys which stopped the French dead in their tracks. They quickly recovered to repulse a massed assault from infantry; and when the rest of the Hessians, Hanoverians and Prussians came to their aid, victory was theirs.

One of the six British regiments who helped the allies win the Battle of Minden on August 1, 1759, was the 20th Foot which became The Lancashire Fusiliers. On each anniversary of the battle, which they called Minden Day, this regiment, wherever they were, took to celebrating the victory with ritual which has become traditional.

It began at Reveille with drummers and fifers marching round the barracks playing The Minden March. Each drummer wore in his headress a red and primrose-yellow rose. While advancing towards the enemy that summer day in 1759 the troops are said to have picked wild roses and stuck them in their hats. On each Minden Day the drums and the drum-major's staff were also decorated with roses of these regimental colours arranged in a pattern making XX—the 20th.

In the officers' mess at the depot hung a portrait of the CO of the 20th Foot at Minden, Colonel William Kingsley, painted by Sir Joshua Reynolds, as a major-general. Every officer who had not already done so at a previous Minden Day, had to eat a rose handed to him in a silver finger bowl filled with champagne. Only then was he considered a full-blooded Lancashire Fusilier.

At the end of the Minden Day Dinner in the mess, The Drums (later accompanied by the band) marched round the table playing The Minden March. As they left the dining room the door was closed before the bass drummer could make his exit with the others. Before he was 'released' he had to make a speech. Traditionally pithy and bawdy, this ended with the bass drummer drinking the health of the officers, clicking his heels and being shown the door, which this time was held open for him. The Royal Regiment of Fusiliers maintain the Minden Day tradition to-day.

The Royal Northumberland Fusiliers, who since 1968 have also been part of The Royal Regiment of Fusiliers, make St George's Day, April 23, the occasion for celebrating the defeat of the French at the Battle of Wilhelmstahl on June 24 1762. In this battle the 5th Foot, as they were then known, forced the whole French Regiment d'Acquitaine and five regiments of Grenadiers to lay down their arms and surrender their colours, of which they took possession. To mark the event a flag of silk gosling green, a memento of the French colour, embroidered with a design showing St George and the Dragon, was taken on parade each St George's Day carried by a regimental drummer and borne on with the rest of The Drums for the beating of Assembly. For this it was called The Drummer's Colour.

'The Drummers Boy's Dream' by F J Shields

All the artillery trains formed after the dispersal of the guns used in Flanders on their return to England in 1698 included Kettledrummers and Kettledrivers for the massive horse-drawn carriages on which they were mounted.

The kettledrummer for the artillery train which went to Holland in March 1702 was paid 3s a day and his driver 1s 6d, which stayed the going rate for some time. A kettlerummer accompanied the artillery train which sailed to Catalonia in Spain in 1709. The brass ordance put at the disposal of the Duke of Marlborough in August 1715 'in consequence of the [Jacobite ?] rebellion' not only had a three shilling a day kettledrummer and driver but four one and six a day side-drummers.

In the revised establishment of the two companies of artillery raised in 1716 which George I ordered in 1720, there were two side-drummers at 1s a day. The first to enlist was eight year old Joseph Brome—young enough, but twice the age of Joseph Eliot who had joined a regiment in 1804 when he was only four. Brome rose to be a lieutenant-general but he never grew very tall. When he was Commandant of Woolwich Garrison he one day paid an official visit to the Warren (the Royal Arsenal). The guard turned out and presented arms, and a drummer beat two ruffles. Whereupon the little general left his party to walk over to the surprised

INFANTRY DRUMMERS—PAST AND PRESENT.

drummer and told him off for his inefficient performance. He snatched the drum away, passed the suspending belt over his own neck and put on a virtuoso demonstration of how it should have been done. Finishing with two dramatic ruffles, he handed back the instrument to its owner with the words 'There you young dog, that's the way I used to drum when I was a drummer.'

At the funeral of the Duke of Marlborough on August 9, 1722 a kettledrum carriage drawn by two horses with kettledrummer and driver drove between two six-pounders and the Master Artificer. Twenty one years later The Royal Regiment of Artillery consisted of eight companies and each had two kettledrummers. The next year two more companies were added and a Cadet Company. The ten companies with their 20 drummers served in Gibraltar, Minorca, Newfoundland, Louisburg as well as in Britain. Why did they take these cumbrous kettledrums and their even more cumbrous carriages with them on these overseas campaigns? A clue is given in the regimental order issued at Herrenthout in June 1747. It required the kettledrummer 'to mount the kettledrum carriage every night half an hour before the sunsett and beat till gun-fireing'. To what end?

In Flanders, where they appeared for the last time in the field in 1748, kettle-drums were carried on what amounted to a triumphal car ornamented and gilded, drawn by *six* white horses, with the Ordnance flag in front. On the march their place was in front of the flag-gun and behind the Artillery front-guard. In camp they sat in front of the quarters of the Duke of Cumberland, the Commander-in-Chief, surrounded by cannon.

The 14 artillery companies established by 1748 had 26 drummers *and fifers*—the latter taught by the Hanoverian John Ulrich. The large oil painting by David Morier of the Royal Artillery in the Low Countries in 1748 (now in the National Army Museum on loan from the Royal Collection and reproduced here by gracious permission of Her Majesty the Queen) shows a company spread out on the right bank of the river Roer outside Roermond. The Duke of Cumberland's army is known to have camped there in April of that year. In the foreground of the picture is the kettledrum carriage with its cargo. The dress of the kettledrummer is not military but court dress. It is that of to-day's state trumpeters and drummers of the Household Cavalry, and of the drum-majors of the Brigade of Guards. The driver's is that of to-day's royal coachmen and postillions.

A fifer wearing a tall mitre cap, with his fife case at his right side beside his dog, sits at the bottom left hand corner on a drum. On the right of him sitting on the ground is a side-drummer with his sword upright between his legs, his drum sling worn over his right shoulder. On his cap are the arms of the Board of Ordnance which controlled the RA until 1857 when the Royal Regiment of Artillery became part of the Army. His uniform is scarlet with blue facings, the reverse of the ordinary regimental uniform, and is laced with the so-called Royal Lace of yellow with a blue stripe.

The five companies of artillery plus cadets which George II reviewed at Woolwich in 1753 included a drum-major, ten drummers, a fife-major and five fifers. The two battalions of Royal Artillery in the West Indies had 47 drummers in 1757.

But when in 1759 the Artillery was divided into independent batteries or brigades and so, as Henry Farmer put it, had ceased to march in one column, the kettledrums were abolished. The fine carriage and drums paraded in the Duke of Marlborough's funeral procession was deposited in the ground floor armoury of the Tower of London. When they were destroyed in a fire in 1841 replicas of the drums and the carriage were made which can still be seen to-day.

Artillery Kettledrums and Carriage, 1700.

How old were the drummers in David Morier's painting of 1748? Young enough not to object to being called boys? The Little Drummer Boy in F J Shields's picture and many other popular prints was not entirely fictitious, though the cherub look gave little impression of the turbulence of their lives. The legend was compounded by romantic stories like J W Fortescue's *The Drummers Coat* about a child's yellow uniform which found its way to Bracefort Hall in the Devonshire village of Ashacombe.

The Drummer Boy dates back to the early eighteenth century, though just when he entered the scene is not clear. Jo Brome becoming a drummer boy at eight was not exceptional but the more normal age was between ten and 12. He must after all have been able to carry a regulation side-drum – there were no 'boy's sizes' like cricket bats. They were not mascots but functional members of the regiment.

It was as a drummer boy that very many started their military career, and it was a way encouraged by the recruiters. Most of them were the sons of regular serving men born in the barracks. Their whole childhood was spent with the regiment; their world was the parade ground, the barrack room. Barracks to take the place of billets was an eighteenth century development. The children born to soldiers who had received permission to marry and lived in with their wives were known as Barrack Rats. They played, slept and ate in the barrack room which was their nursery. The army fed and educated them. Both in the army, the quickest way to become of it was to stop watching what went on and start *doing* it – officially and for pay, however irregular. And at as early an age as the colonel would permit. How better to ease his way into the rougher aspects of army life than by learning to beat a drum and becoming a Drummer Boy?

He was given a uniform which at once changed his relationship with the man whom perhaps he had worshipped from afar but had now to be obeyed rather than admired. Following the instructions of the Regimental Drum-Major in drum beating and the basics of military discipline now over-shadowed all else.

Some had ambitions of becoming a fully-fledged, grown-up side-drummer which they could at 18, able to undertake the parleying, and made sure they learnt the necessary languages while mastering the difficult technique of beating camp calls and accompanying the fifes on the march and ceremonial parades.

Others like John Shipp could not wait for their eighteenth birthday to become an infantryman proper, after years of drumming and blowing fifes and bugles. He was set on improving himself. He got his captain to teach him how to read and write, and after a year he was keeping the company's account books.

I then begged of the captain that I might be removed from the drummers to the ranks. I did not like the appellation drum-boy. As I have seen many a man riding post, who was at least sixty years old, so, if a drummer had attained the age of Methuselah, he would never acquire any other title than drum-boy ... In about a week after having made this request I was transferred from the drummers room and promoted to the rank of corporal ... This was promotion indeed – three steps in one day! From drum-boy to private, from a battalion company to the Light Bobs; and from private to corporal!

He never became a lieutenant-general like Joseph Brome but settled for a lieutenancy in the 87th Foot.

Though a Drummer Boy was paid less than a Drummer, the latter received more than a Private. So to abandon The Drums in which he would never become an officer meant a short term sacrifice in the hope of preferment in the long term. It was what the Army hoped would happen. The Government were finding it difficult to find enough suitable young men to fight the revolutionary armies of France – as every drummer who took part in recruiting knew well. They hoped that a more fruitful source of material for the regular army would be volunteers in the county militia units, one regiment of which was attached to each regiment of the line and was expected to be a feeder to it.

In 1792 the Government tried having men embodied and enrolled for the Militia by ballot, casting lots in each community for those who would have to join and fill the required quota. Henry Cockburn, who later became a Scottish Lord of Justiciary, knew well how 'the terror of the ballot' filled the ranks,

> **while duty, necessity and especially the contagion of the times, supplied officers. The result was we became a military population. Any able-bodied man of whatever rank who was not a volunteer or a local militia-man, had to explain or apologise for his singularity.**

The Government, who knew the ballot system would be unpopular, provided a let-out clause by which a man whose name had come out of the hat was allowed to send a substitute whom he probably had to pay. The Member of Parliament for Coventry, Mr P Moore, told the House of Commons in June 1804 that in the Tower Hamlets Militia hardly ten men were serving personally; all the rest were substitutes who had agreed to serve for five years or for the duration of the war.

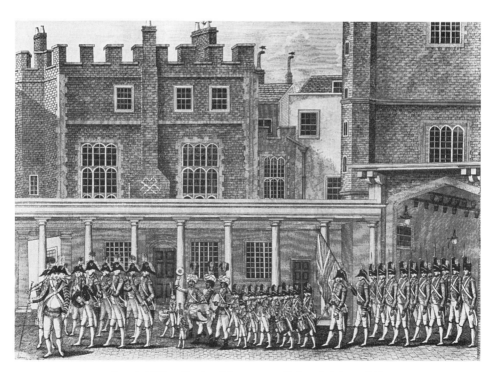

Guards Military Band and Drummers at St James's Palace, 1790.

They consider themselves as serving not His Majesty but as substitutes for the parochial inhabitants . . . Several constituents of mine have applied lately for a discharge with a view to getting a more extended service or a renewal of the bounty – the first man who made the application was taken up, tried by a court martial and sentenced to receive 300 lashes. By my intercession the lashes were remitted by taking away 295 of the 300 lashes. I mention this circumstance to show how difficult it is to get men even for the regular army.

The Annual Register of 1810 recorded how the 'evil of the ballot system' reached a climax when 'last week £66 was paid out at Plymouth for a substitute for the militia. One man went on condition of receiving 4s a day during the war and another then sold himself for 7s 3d per 1b'.

The following year the method of obtaining men for the general militia was reorganised so that recruiting was once more By Beat of Drum and not by ballot.

In the meantime ambitious drummer boys like John Shipp, who wished to make a career of soldiering, helped to leaven the 'scum of the earth' who marched behind the Iron Duke who, with the allies, steadily repelled the well-drilled armies of the Disturber of Europe in the first decade and a half of the nineteenth century.

MORE RECENT YEARS

Chapter 5

5   High in Spirit, in Excellent Moral Condition

Massing Drums; Stretching the Establishment; More Trophies; Arroyo dos Molinos, Albuera, Waterloo; Samuel Potter, manual writer and drum maker; Bass and Tenor Drums; Metal shells for side-drums; Bugles take over Camp Calls; Drums and Bagpipes; The Crimean War; George Potter catalogue for 1885.

Bonaparte knew the effect which military music could have on the morale of a body of men. The French had large bands of brass instruments and large *batteries* of drums. Court musicians devised compositions for both of them. The *batteries* beat on their own or with fifes; but were at their most impressive when they beat the electrifying *Batterie Fanfare* with the band. Raw young soldiers of British regiments who found themselves in a strange country in the strange situation of 'going to war' far removed from the picture of army life painted by the recruiting sergeant, were terrified by the noise of the massed drums of advancing French regiments, the like of which they had never heard in all their lives.

Unlike the British, the French advanced in column, massing all their drummers in the centre, and then deployed into line with a great spread of troops – a movement which never failed to intrepidate all who watched it. The drums beating their *Pas de Charge* was a tactic on which Bonaparte relied to give the maximum effect. He valued it highly – and the person who sounded it.

Shortly after he had become virtual dictator of France as First Consul under the constitution of November 1799 (Brumaire), he was reviewing the troops who that summer had won a great victory at Zurich against the Russians.

The great man stopped in front of a 16 year old drummer boy.
'So, my boy, it was you who beat the charge at Zurich, was it? And with a bullet through your right arm?'
The boy blushed.
'Yes, general'.
'And it was you too, I understand, who showed great presence of mind at Weser?'
'Yes, general'.
'Well, it is up to me to pay what the country owes you. I shall not give you a drum stick of honour. I shall present you with a sabre of honour. I appoint you a Non-Commissioned Officer in the First Consul's Guard. Go on as you have begun, and I shall take care of you'.
'Then' continued the contemporary report of this encounter 'the First Consul with a pleasant smile touched his hat to the ladies who had been listening to him. The little drummer was as pale as death with emotion, but his face was eloquent'.

Appreciating, from the receiving end, the impact of having the drums of a regiment massed together instead of strung out along the regiment in companies, the British took a leaf out of Bonaparte's book and did the same. From now on The Drums were grouped either at the head or in the middle of a regiment.

The British also came to prize more greatly the ability of military bands to raise morale. At the beginning of the nineteenth century such bands were very small and remained so until the Crimean War – rarely more than ten to 12 players. Hitherto bands had been of the army but not in it. The first official recognition came with the issue in 1803 of an Army Regulation stating:

> **It is His Majesty's pleasure that in regiments having bands of music not more than one private solider of each troop or company shall be permitted to act as musicians; and that one Non Commissioned Officer shall be allowed to act as Master of the Band. These men shall be drilled and instructed in their exercise, and in the case of actual service are to fall in with the respective troops or companies completely armed and accoutred – soldiers first, bandsmen second.**
>
> **His Royal Highness the Commander-in Chief requires general officers commanding districts to communicate above order to several regiments under their command and strictly enforce its observance.**

First to import a complete band were the Coldstream Guards consisting of ten musicians, mostly Germans, who became soldiers and bandsmen. Apart from borrowing their idea of putting The Drums en masse, the British also adopted French military airs. As an alternative to *The British Grenadiers* and *Rule Britannia*, British bands which went to Spain in 1808 with regiments for the Peninsular War played an early French revolutionary song *Ça Ira* (We Will Succeed). In 1793 it

The Queen's Own Hussars drum horse carrying replicas of the silver kettledrums captured at the Battle of Dettingen in 1743.

'The Drum Horse, Royal Scots Greys' by Gilbert Holiday.

had been adopted as the quickstep of the 14th Foot *(The West Yorkshire Regiment)*. But one of the *Instructions for the Drill* (The 18 Manoeuvres) of 1803 discouraged

MUSIC AND DRUMS

The use of music or drums to *regulate* the march in movement of manoeuvre is absolutely forbid, as incompatible with the just and combined movements of any considerable body, and *giving a false aid to the very smallest.* They never persevere in *ordered time,* or in any other, are constantly changing measure, create noise, derange the equality of step, and counteract the very end they are supposed to promote. The *ordered and cadenced march* can be acquired and preserved from the eye and habit alone, and troops must, by great practice, be *so steadied* as to be able to maintain it, even though drums or music of any kind should mark a different time.
[their italics]

Two years later *The Military Companion* was requiring the drum-major to turn his staff 'with an easy air one round so as to keep time and plant it at every fourth pace.' The precise angle at which he held it could convey one of 17 commands without a word being called out. Six years later *Regulations for the Army* for the guidance of drum-majors stipulated

they should be attentive not to deviate in the first trifling degree from the time which will allow, within the minute, the exact number of steps prescribed by HM Regulations.

But the purpose of Drums and Music for *drilling* and parade ground ceremonial no longer applied when the regiment was campaigning. Once the regiment was overseas the value to it of The Drums was greatly enhanced, and for different reasons. And so much so that many commanding officers had no hesitation in stretching the rules to produce a larger volume of sound than they were entitled to. There was an 'establishment' of the number of drummers a regiment could have on its strength, and it was limited by the funds allocated to pay for them. So they could not add to their strength. But many colonels used the money budgetted for, say, 400 privates to be paid to 395 privates and five drummer boys, who on their returns however would be shown as privates. They were known as Contingency Men. By the fiddle of turning Duty Men into Additional Drummers, the colonels hoped no one would notice. Not all of them got away with it.

When the 2nd Battalion of the 89th Foot (which with the 87th became the Royal Irish Fusiliers) were sent to ease the pressure on Cadiz in 1810 and attack Fuengirola, all but 230 of them were taken prisoner. When this remnant were inspected at Gibraltar, the Inspecting Officer told them they were not fit for service. There was a marked shortage of officers, he noted, but no shortage of musicians: 'Music and Drummers of forty-four people'. He ordered the number to be reduced to 15.

The following year of town of Tarifa near Gibraltar was invested by the French whose cannon knocked a hole in its wall. On New Year's Eve some 2,000 grenadiers attacked but lost their way. Instead of landing up at the hole they arrived at the main gate of the town where the 87th Foot were waiting for them with grapeshot and cannon fire. Over the roaring of the firing the 87th's Drums and Fifes played *Garryowen to Glory Boys* which, to hasten the retreat of the French though the mud, they later changed to *St Patrick's Day*. They needed all the additional drummers they could muster to let the joyful beating and blowing to be heard above the din of *that* fracas.

At this same Battle of Tarifa a colonel of Valencian troops recognised the number and crest of his regiment on the bass drum being beaten by the drummer of the 28th Foot which had captured it in Minorca in 1798. But so far from wanting it back, the Spanish colonel said he was glad to see it in such good hands. A sense of fraternity among military musicians often transcended temporary national animosity.

The 34th Foot (later the 1st Battalion The Border Regiment) who captured the drums and drum-major's staff of the 34th Foot of the French army at Arroyo dos Molinos in October 1811 were granted a special battle honour.

DRUM-MAJORS OF INFANTRY OF THE LINE—1808, ROYAL ARTILLERY—1825, AND 26TH FOOT (CAMERONIANS), 1852.

In 1800 a General Order had introduced the 'shako' cap as a regular headress for British infantry, a cylindrical affair made of black lacquered leather as wide at the top as at the bottom with a large brass plate in front, worn by drummers as well as privates. To honour their capture of the French 34th along with their drums, the British 34th were allowed to wear a red and white tuft on their shakos. The remainder of the infantry, except for the Rifles and the Light Infantry, wore a white one. When in 1845 wearing a red and white tuft became standard for all infantry and the 34th lost their distinction, the regiment was granted the battle honour 'Arroyo dos Molinos'. To commemorate the exploit The Border Regiment trooped the drums and drum-major's staff of the French 34th every anniversary of the action. The youngest drummer boy carried the French staff dressed as a drum-major. This custom is maintained to-day by 1st Battalion The King's Own Royal Border Regiment.

The action took place only five months after 'the most murderous and sanguinary conflict' of the Peninsular War, the Battle of Albuera, in which however no French trophies were captured. It was the battle in which William Inglis the brigade commander cried as he fell mortally wounded 'Die hard, the 57th!' – after which The Middlesex Regiment, successors to the heroic 57th Foot, have always been known as The Diehards. The Victorian artist Lady Butler chose it for her famous picture *Steady the Drums and Fifes*! commissioned by The Diehards in 1896. Gregory Blaxland, the historian of The Middlesex Regiment, says she portrayed the drummers because their lemon-yellow tunics gave her relief from the perpetual scarlet of her other commissioned works. In fact, he adds, The Drums suffered only one killed and three wounded at Albuera, and were less exposed than she depicts. The model for the small drummer boy without a headress in the front line was Martin Butler, the artist's youngest son; and for the Grenadier with his hand on his head Patrick Butler, his elder brother, who was to join the army and rise to the rank of colonel.

At that time The Drums of the 57th will have played the music which Major General Sir Manley Power, commander of the 2nd Brigade found in a French camp. The score was adapted to become the regiment's own march and was called *Sir Manley Power*. It survived as such until 1859 when the regiment was stationed in Richmond Barracks, Dublin. The GOC took exception to it on the grounds that it was 'all drum and damned nonsense'. He ordered the 57th's CO to find another. It surfaced again however in 1896 when the 1st Battalion adopted it as a quickstep.

The Drums were more in evidence as time keepers and on the march than in the battles of the Peninsular War however. Sailing up the river Tagus in the heat of the Portuguese summer of July 1809 just after the battle of Talavera, Captain Moyle Sherer recollected:

Our drum beat two hours before dawn of day and at an early hour we reached Niza; not however before the sun had acquired such fierce and burning power as to strike me down thrice in a very few minutes.

The following autumn at Almeyrim on the left bank of the Tagus, right opposite French army headquarters at Santarem, they relied on the drummers to alert them to any danger.

Although we remained nearly three months unmolested by the enemy and inactive ourselves, we could none of us feel certain we should continue so. We should never have been surprised had the alarm drum at midnight roused us from our beds; and the idea that this was possible took from the insipidity of life in other respects monotonous.

There was no need or occasion for drum beating or fife playing to keep them together on the long six league march in November 1810 through Alhandra and Villa Franca to Caregada. It was their singing that will have made their line of march 'all gaiety and animation' in pursuit of a retreating enemy. But every now and again the colonel would call to his drummer 'Sound the Halt!' The boy would beat The Halt, and each company drummer in the column behind would hear it and beat a Halt too. Knowing the captain was unlikely to know the meaning of the beat, the company drummer would turn to him and say 'That's the halt, sir!', and the company commander would give the necessary order.

In forming up the regiments that Sunday June 18, 1815 for the final showdown with Bonaparte, now the second-time-round Emperor of the French and Commander-in-Chief of the French Army of the North, on the hills above Mont St Jean, the regimental and company drummers and fifers played their part – and the bands which they accompanied.

Frederick Hopkins of the 33rd Foot recollected (in 1870) how at Quatre Bras before the Battle of Waterloo,

the bugles sounded the Advance, the band struck up *The British Grenadiers* and the brigade moved off with increased alacrity, high in spirit and in excellent moral condition to meet the enemy.

When the French army had been routed and Napoleon's dream of a come-back had been finally shattered, there was a nice gesture from the Prussians under Prince Blucher whom the Duke of Wellington recognised had played so vital a part in achieving victory. Troop Sergeant Major Cotton of the 7th Hussars has described how

When our gallant infantry finally broke the Emperor's Old Guard we followed them until we came up with the Prussians, and as they passed us their bands play 'God Save The King!' which soul-stirring compliment we returned with hearty cheers.

And when it was all over and the man whom the British had never recognised as anything other than First Consul, had been removed to the island of St Helena, The Drums, along with every other part of the British Army, were able to relax. But they saw to it that they maintained the customary high standard in the execution of their difficult art. In his report the Inspecting Officer who inspected the 28th Foot in 1816 had no hesitation in stating:

> **The drummers appeared perfect in the different beats of the Drum and to be active and attentive to their duty. I thought the Musicians played too quick time, although their Commanding Officer assured me they had been practised on their Plummets.**

But perhaps in using these phrases to describe the performance of what became The Gloucestershire Regiment, the Inspecting Officer was applying rule book terms, not that that meant that the drummers were any less efficient than the words signified. His report on the 61st Foot stated:

> **The Drummers are perfect in their beats of the drum, and attentive to their duty. The Musicians play in correct time and are trained and fit for the ranks. There is not anyone who is not clothed and who does not do his duty as a soldier.**

Drums for the Crimea.

The side-drums which the drummers of British regiments carried with them across the plains of the Iberian Peninsular, North America and India, through France and Holland, were made in small workshops in the City of London and other towns. The names of the craftsmen who fashioned these necessarily robust but musically sound instruments have largely been lost or forgotten. That of Potter however has not only survived in memory but the firm bearing that name is to-day still an active supplier of military drums to customers all over the world.

Samuel Potter was probably around 38 when in 1810 he wrote the namual *The Art of Beating The Drum with Camp, Garrison and Street Duty by note,* Dedicated by Permission to HRH Duke of Kent. He was, or had been, a sergeant and drum-major in the Coldstream Regiment of Foot Guards which he had joined, presumably as a drummer boy, at the age of 14 in 1786. He claimed to come from a family of flute makers dating back to the sixteenth century.

A Richard Potter was one of the best known flute makers in Europe. He came from Mitcham in Surrey but in 1740 was apprenticed to a turner in the City of London called Bickerton. After his marriage to Mary Huddleston in 1754 the two of them went to live in Cripplegate. Later they acquired a house in Pemberton Row, Gough Square. He is said to have made an early six-key flute of new design. When he died in 1806 his flute-making business, R Potter & Son, was carried on by his second son William Henry Potter who probably made drums and other musical instruments as well, but in any case closed it down for good in 1837 and died a wealthy man in 1848. Richard Potter's eldest son Richard Huddleston Potter was for nearly 40 years organist at St Brides Church, Fleet Street.

What relationship Drum-Major Samuel Potter had to Flute-maker Richard Potter has not been established, but the two of them were probably cousins of some sort. Samuel Potter always alleged that his line of the Potter family also made flutes in London in the eighteenth century and in 1742 had a workshop at the sign of The Three Squirrels in Fleet Street. Be that as it may, by 1800 Samuel had become not only an accomplished drummer and fifer (flautist) but the composer of a piece of music for Two Fifes and a Bugle Horn published in that year. When *The Art of Beating the Drum* was published in 1810 he was an acknowledged authority.

For a long time, he said, he had been studying in what manner to write the Duty of the side-drum by Note, 'as that part of Drum Beating is so very intricate'. He apologised for having to talk about Appogiaturas which he used for Flams and Drags, and the Shake for Rolls and Staccato, but he hoped such technical terms 'would not be deemed too troublesome', as he had avoided them as much as possible. He then proceeded to give straightforward instruction.

Before a boy starts practising a drum place him perfectly upright and place his left heel in the hollow of his right foot. Put the drum sticks into his hands, the right stick to be grasped by the whole hand 2½ inches from the top, similar to grasping a sword or stick when going to play Back-sword. The left hand one to be held between the thumb and the forefinger close in the hollow, leaving the top as much protruding resembling a pen when going to write.

The instructor is then to sling the drum on the boy's neck 'being careful the Drum-Carriage [the supporting strap] is of moderate length, the drum bearing on the left thigh so when the knee is bent the drum balances on it.' Before learning the Long Roll he must take up the first position with his elbows level with his ears, 'the left elbow as much to the front as the boy can bear without pain'. In learning Rolls, Flams, Drags, Paradiddles and the rest, he must begin them very slowly and increase moderately to the quickness required. If the boy made a mistake, however trifling, he must immediately leave off and begin again. Otherwise 'he will get a bad habit that will make his drum beating a pain to himself and appear like labour to those who see him beat; whereas if he keeps to this rule he will learn to beat the drum with ease to himself, and it will appear slight to those who see him as it ought to be, the pride of every drummer to beat his Duty with an Air and Spirit'.

The Long Roll was the foundation of drum beating. A side-drum only had one note and he was going to write it on the music sheet as the note C in the bass cleff – in the second space from the bottom:

The Long Roll was known by a Shake and a Pause marked over the note.

Once the boy had mastered that, he should be taught the Seven Stroke Roll, then the Eleven Stroke Roll, followed by the Open Flam, the Ten Stroke Roll, the Close Flam from Hand to Hand, a Flam and a Stroke from Hand to Hand, a Flam and a Faint from Hand to Hand, a Faint and Flam from Hand to Hand, the Drag, the Drag and Stroke.

The boy was now ready to learn the plain beating of The Grenadiers March, the Drummers Call, the Troop Page, the Serjeants Call, the Non-Commissioned Officers Call, the Retreat, the Taptoo, the General. He could then progress to The Mother (or Five Stroke Roll from Hand to Hand), the three Camp Taps and the Salute when receiving or delivering the colours.

> **The Camp Taps is the First Signal on the Drum; it must be repeated from Right to Left of the Line by a drummer of each regiment and return back from Left to Right previous to the Reveille. The Mother and Three Camps and Scotch Reveile to be beat all three in Ordinary Time.**

In the year the manual was published Samuel Potter decided to benefit from the acclaim which it received in military circles by acquiring a drum-making business and setting up as a supplier of drums and fifes to the British Army. In 1810 therefore he bought a firm (his ancestor's) which had a workshop and retail premises at the sign of The Three Squirrels in Fleet Street making and selling musical instruments including drums. As a regular solider he could not engage in trade, let alone as one who did business with his employer, so he had the company registered in the name of the son who had been born that year – Henry Potter & Co.

Five years later Samuel was living off Vincent Square behind Westminster Abbey, and published a second manual *The Art of Playing the Fife:* and in 1817 *Manual for Drums, Fifes and Bugles.* He left the army in 1817 and from then to his death in 1837 he lived in King Street Westminster. His son Henry Potter carried on the London business which moved to 2 Bridge Street and then to 30 Charing Cross, and in 1856 opened a branch in the new military camp in Aldershot.

Henry's three sons William, Henry (2) and George all become involved in the business on a basis of equal shares until 1872, when George bought the Aldershot branch from his two brothers and set it up as a separate company under the name of George Potter & Co. The two firms under separate managements – Henry Potter & Co of Charing Cross and later West Street, and George Potter & Co of Aldershot – competed with each other in the same market without any apparent damage to either of them. And they continued to do so even when they were re-united after George's son, Major J G R Potter, inherited the London Company.

The instruments supplied to the British Army by Potter and other firms such as Cornelius Ward of 36 Titchfield Street, Tottenham Court Road, John Kohler of Henrietta Street, Covent Garden and Robert Horn, were not only side-drums but the big bass drums which came in with 'Janissary Music', the *davul* played with a double-headed stick on one side and a metal rod or brush on the other. The Janissaries were the Turkish *Yeni cherik* of regularly formed regiments with officers and non-commissioned officers, as well as staff musicians, all uniformed and barracked. The influence of this first 'standing army' was not fully felt in the West until Austrian troops marched into Vienna preceded by a Turkish band in 1741. By 1770 almost every European army had introduced Turkish percussion instruments into their regimental bands including the bass drum and the Jingling Johnny or Turkish Crescent.

> **Turkish marches** (wrote Henry Farmer) **now crowded into the military music collections published during the last quarter of the century, and they had already been popular with the Drums and Fifes in the two earlier decades ... The instruments themselves were adopted by us via the Germans who were already equipped with their *Janitscharen Musik*. The Royal Artillery Band had a bass drum, cymbals, and tambourine in 1782.**

Henry Potter & Co made a bass drum which was used that Sunday June 18 1815 at Mont St Jean. One the back of one of their 1870 catalogues was the note:

The following may be of interest

A RELIC OF WATERLOO

Bass drum of the reign of George III and used at the battle of Waterloo. By consent of -- Downs Esq, Mayor of Basingstoke 1855, and the committee of M I C B [?] this drum reverted as a business relic of the makers to George Potter & Co of Aldershot.

In those days a bass drum used by The Drums was much wider, perhaps twice as wide as the diameter of its face or head, whereas later the width was greatly reduced until it was half the diameter of the head. The drummer was able to execute his elaborate cross-hand doubling from one side to the other because he did not carry it on his chest but at his waist.

The little marching kettledrum seen in the 1790 engraving of guard mounting at St James's Palace, was replaced in The Drums by the Tenor Drum. The earliest record of a tenor drum being used in Britain is in 1834 by the Royal Artillery Band. It was longer than the ordinary side-drum and its lower head had no 'snares'. Beaten with felt or soft headed drumsticks, the tenor drum had a distinctive subdued tone of its own.

The wearing of leopard skin aprons by bass and tenor drummers is often thought to have been introduced by the negro percussionists who first performed the new Janissary Music. But William Boag, Assistant to the Keeper of the Scottish United Services Museum in Edinburgh, and leading authority on The Drum, believes it started by being a way of using the skins of animals shot by British army officers serving in Africa and India, to which there was frequently fixed an inscribed silver plate giving the date and place of the killing and the name and regiment of the killer.

For some time there was considerable variety in the size of side-drums issued by Ordnance to British infantry regiments – apart, that is, from the new Rifle Regiments which came into being at the beginning of the nineteenth century and as skirmishers did without them. For signalling they used bugles. In the last quarter of the eighteenth century the overall size of the side-drum was reduced to a standard 18 inches by 18 inches, and the height of the hoop (the lip around the head) to two inches. At the time of Waterloo the size was reduced again to 16 inches by 16 inches, though those carried by the Guards and some other regiments at the battle were of the old size.

The French changed their side-drums from wood to metal early in the eighteenth century, but a regulation made in the reign of George II stipulated that the side-drum beaten by British regimental drummers should remain of wood, generally ash. The overlapping ends of the shell were secured by nails or tacks – the Nail Board – arranged in elaborate patterns to hide the fact that there was a join. The side-drums of the British army did not change to metal until the beginning of the nineteenth century. They had had snares – a series of fine cords – across the bottom head for a long time, probably since the seventeenth century, and now, made of fine gut and coming into play on the new brass shell, they gave the side-drum a sound which was of exceptional resonance.

These side-drums wore well. One which Henry Potter & Co made for a Volunteer Regiment in 1830 was beaten to celebrate the passing of the Reform Bill in 1832, the coronation of Queen Victoria in 1838 and the declaration of peace after the Crimean War, and Sergeant George Ricketts was praising it for surviving to 1890.

Kettledrums for the cavalry, in which the firm of Kohler specialised, had always been of metal of course – those presented to the Life Guards by King William IV in Windsor Great Park in 1831 were of silver. A kettledrum carried on one man's back, and beaten by a kettledrummer walking behind him, featured in Queen Victoria's wedding procession of 1838.

Presentation of drums to the St George's Volunteers.

In contrast to glittering ceremonies such as these, traditional rituals of a more melancholy nature were still in a drummer's repertoire of varied duties.

Corporal Ryder never forgot the day he had to parade with the 32nd Foot in India in the 1840s for the execution of a private who in a drunken fit had struck their commanding officer in the face with his cap. On arriving at Meerut the regiment received a number of men who had chosen not to return to England with their regiments but stay on in India in the army, and been posted to the 32nd. The drunken and mutinous behaviour of these old campaigners was a great worry to Colonel Hill the 32nd's CO, and he had to caution the whole regiment that striking a superior officer was punishable by death. Four men were court-martialled and shot. Ryder witnessed the execution of one of them, a man who had been with the 9th Lancers and had hit Colonel Hill.

The whole regiment paraded in the form of a three-sided square, the open side being left for the shot to pass through when the soldiers fired.

After the first dawn I could see the party stand with the prisoner, when they were ordered to proceed in the following manner: first the provost with his arms reversed; then the band and drummers playing the 'Dead March', the drums being muffled with black; next the firing party with arms reversed; then the coffin borne by four men; next to this the prisoner in company of the minister praying, and his comrade on the left of him flanked by a man on either side with swords, the escort following.

They started from the left; the band played the dismal and solemn march which made my blood run cold. As he passed his own regiment he bade his officers and the men farewell ... The minister had hold of his arm, but he walked with a firm step, keeping the step to the drum, and with the party.

The bitter Drumming Out ceremonial persisted for the soldier discharged with ignominy and good riddance, but there were jollier occasions for drummers at hearty farewell parties for popular soldiers who had served the regiment well and it was a matter of 'Sorry to see you go'. Surrounded by friends wishing him good luck in Civvy Street, the departing soldier fell in behind The Drums and was led to the barrack gates to the music of the regimental march. Outside they all rallied round and shook hands with him while drums and fifes played *Auld Lang Syne*. Someone called for three hearty cheers and off he went.

The degrading corporal punishment duties became less and less after flogging diminished following an order of November 9 1858, and was abolished in time of peace by an amendment to a clause in the Mutiny Bill of April 1868. The last floggings in the British army took place in 1880, and the punishment was finally abolished altogether by the Army Discipline Act of 1881.

Gradually less and less reliance was placed on The Drums for signalling in the British army. In 1798 the Secretary of State for War ordered an enquiry into the use of the drum, fife and bugle in an attempt to standardise procedures and signalling codes which could be understood by *all* regiments. To sort the matter out and advise them on how to go about it, they commissioned James Hyde who, besides being a trumpet player in the orchestra of the Covent Garden Opera House, was Trumpet Major to the gentlemen who had volunteered for the Westminster Dragoons, one of London's many yeomanry regiments. Hyde made a collection of every drum, trumpet and bugle call in use and put them on a proper basis.

Bugles took over from drums for Camp and Field Calls as the means of broadcasting time checks and commands largely because they could be heard more easily and could sound more than one note. The Rifle Regiments already had a long tradition of marching to unaccompanied bugles. The Bugles and The Band played together, and many marches were written for such a combination.

Originally the horn of the wild ox (for which word was once 'bugle'), The Bugle-Horn was replaced by a re-designed brass replica of a horn and given a mouthpiece. There could be no doubt that the noise that issued from it was the blast of a bugle and not musket fire for which a drum beat could be mistaken. In more and more regiments of the line signalling was undertaken by bugle calls. So that regiments fighting alongside one another could tell which bugled order was intended for them and not their comrades on the right, the calls came to be identified by being preceded by a Regimental Bugle Call.

In the Artillery the drum was discarded as a signal and duty instrument in favour of the bugle or trumpet around 1848. There was a Drum and Fife 'band' at Woolwich however until 1856, the year Sir Fenwick Williams the commandant turned it into a Bugle Band.

By the time British regiments were being sent to fight in the Crimea in 1854 most military drummers were also buglers. There were men and boys who could beat a drum, play a fife and blow a bugle. Some probably were only drum-beaters and buglers; others maybe were purely fifers. But in the line regiments there were no separate corps of buglers who played nothing else. 'The Drums' remained the section of the regiment, quite separate from The Band, which consisted of drum-beaters, fifers and bugler/trumpeters. And Drums and Fifes retained their indispensable role on the march. Bugle Marches were written for bugles and drums, which the Light Infantry still march to to-day, but fifes could play sophisticated tunes beyond the range of bugles.

Bagpipes were not played with drums till later – probably the 1860s. Due to the Duke of Gordon's wife who raised the Gordon Highlanders? William Boag considers it may have been the Govan Police Band who first had the two playing together, and the Army copied them. Or was it the other way round? However that may be, when Pipes started being played with Drums for parades and in marching by Scottish Regiments, an entirely new style of side-drumming developed, which was never adopted south of the Border. It was a complicated Scottish Style which did not reach maturity until the early 1930s. Drums being beaten with fifes could get by on a series of relatively simple beats, but it was another matter having to accompany bagpipes for which a large number of marches of an intricate nature had already been written. The simple, standard, traditional beatings taught to military drummers 'did not sit nicely with them'. For this a new drum beat annotation was devised (not by the Army) which, instead of the five-line musical stave, had a single line with the strokes for the drummer's right hand noted above it and those for his left hand below.

In 1854 certain Scots regiments were given permission to have five pipers and a Pipe Major; and in 1881 *all* Highland Regiments received that permission, though it was not until 1922 that Irish regiments got it. Many writers have used 'fife' when they meant 'pipe' (bagpipe), but it is likely that all Scottish Regiments had Drums and Fifes as well as Pipes. As late as the beginning of the twentieth century there is reason to believe that the Royal Scots Fusiliers still had fifes on their charge as well as pipes. There were Drum and Fife duty calls, and calls for beating on the drum only and calls to be played solely on the fife.

PRESENTATION OF COLOURS TO THE 93RD (SUTHERLAND) HIGHLANDERS IN THE QUEEN'S PARK, EDINBURGH.

Drums and fifes played regiments to action in the Crimean War which broke out in 1854. But Field Marshal Lord Raglan, who lost an arm at Waterloo and commanded the British Forces in Crimea, banned all military music for a time. However, as Henry Farmer relates, 'the drums and fifes never ceased their battering and tootling to the great joy of the rank and file of the army'.

There was an outcry against Raglan's decision, and William Howard Russell, the intrepid correspondent who covered the war for *The Times*, told his readers about the drums and fifes of the Foot Guards

who kept the whole place alive last night and cheered the drenched Rifle picquets far above the bay on the misty mountain tops by the familiar squeaks of 'Cheer, boys, cheer!' and 'Willikins and his Dinah', aided by a rattling chorus.

The drums the Foot Guards took to the Crimea had a brass shell measuring 14 inches by 11½ inches with two-inch wooden hoops of ash, calfskin heads, and white hemp rope. They had eight buff braces and six or more gut strand snares. Apart from a one inch variation in the 1900s the Guards stuck to this specification which became known as the 'Guards Regulation Pattern Drum'.

Raglan bowed to the clamour, and military bands were re-mobilised after the Battle of Sebastopol – and played at Raglan's funeral after he had died of dysentery in June 1855. 'The Drums' had not been affected by Raglan's ban, their role as ever was more than just providing music, though they were still stylishly dressed. The 17 drummers on the establishment of The Buffs at this time – eight companies with two in each plus a drum-major – wore smart single breasted tunics, dark blue serge trousers and black ankle boots. But drum-majors were robbed of their over-fancy uniforms and made to wear those of a staff-sergeant which was not entirely lacking in colour however. It was a double-breasted scarlet coatee with yellow facings and silver lace, buttons and epaulettes. A drawing of the drum-major of the 26th or Cameronian Regiment of 1852 showed him wearing a uniform such as this with the 'Mullet' or five-pointed star of the Earl of Angus on his drum belt which was the regimental badge. On his head was a bearskin cap with a long scarlet hackle coiling right over it.

The process of cutting the drum-major down to size was taken a step further in 1881 when he was deprived of his title and re-named Sergeant Drummer. 'Drum-Major' was thought to be too high sounding, and it was not restored until 1928. Queen Victoria inspired a Brigade of Guards order that drum-majors were not to spin and twirl their staffs as was done in other regiments. The rank of Fife Major was abolished in 1848, though for four years an NCO continued to carry out the duties of a fife major without having the rank.

In 1855 drummers stopped wearing coatees and were given tunics. They continued to wear the 'wings' on their shoulders, worn by 'Flank' companies, which had now disappeared. The Flank Companies were abolished in 1862, the year in which for the first time drummers received formal military training. In the Crimean War the only weapon carried by a drummer was a specially made sword. But the distinctive mark of the drummers of the Infantry of the Line was to be 'Crown Lace', the red crown introduced in 1872 and worn on the lace or tape of all infantry of the line in place of the previously worn regimental lace. It was worn on full dress tunics up to 1939. Drummers of the Foot Guards however wore blue fleur-de-lys, not Crown Lace. A sword had been the personal weapon of the drummer since the sixteenth century, as seen. In 1857 a drummer's sword with a 19 inch blade was introduced which they wore until 1903 when it became obsolete.

The exception to all this were the drummers of The Royal Fusiliers who had distinctive swords presented to them by HRH the Duke of Kent in 1790 which 200 years later are still worn sometimes by members of the band of The Royal Regiment of Fusiliers to-day.

As Richard Powell has pointed out, despite all the campaigning of the period, 1881-1914 saw the sustaining of the most magnificent full dress uniforms. and the development of many drummers' accoutrements besides swords such as dress cords, regimental staves, the acorns worn on Foot Guards' staves when drum majors wore state dress, the full buff kit and the ticking bag fastened to the drum's side.

It was a time when The Drums beat for anything within the battalion's whim: for church, for welcomes, departures, boxing matches, reveille, football encouragement, tea parties, visiting hospitals, the serjeant major's birthday . . . In addition Foot Guards' drums also effected their share of normal public duties: guard mounting at London and Windsor, drummers with the Bank Picquet and Tower Guard, including the Ceremony of the Keys, state visits, weekly summer retreats for the Royal Hospital Chelsea, and other royal occasions.

The Crimean War provided the first opportunity since Waterloo for regiments to win trophies, among which the enemy's drums were still highly prized. The Russian drum captured by The Royal Berkshire Regiment was brought back to England and beaten by a regimental drummer every week to lead officers into the dining room on Guest Nights. After the regiment captured a German side-drum in the Great War some 60 years later, Rolling In officers on guest nights was performed on both trophies, Russian and German. When the band played *The Roast Beef of Old England* the two drummers led the officers from the ante-room into the dining room. The drummer with the Russian drum went to one side of the table, the one with the German drum to the other side. On reaching the middle they halted but continued beating until all the officers were seated. They then stopped and withdrew.

Though certain ceremonies and usages became obsolete at the latter end of the nineteenth century, The Drums were never in danger of losing their essential functional role in the years of comparative peace which followed the war in the Crimea. Many regiments took the opportunity of spelling out more precisely than hitherto just what those functions were. Standing Orders of the 1st Battalion The 5th Foot (Northumberland Fusiliers) of December 31, 1875 stated:

The Drum-major is under the immediate orders of the Adjutant and is responsible that the drummers, fifers and buglers are instructed in every part of their duty; that they practise regularly and that they take proper care of their instruments.

He must not allow unauthorised drum beating; daily see that guardroom and orderly room clocks showed the same time; see all bugle calls and drum beats were made at the correct hour and were preceded by the battalion call; looked after the Colours and belts and kept them clean; gave the executive command to the band and drums when marching. 'The band and drums will be treated as a company with regard to messing, cooking etc.'

If for any reason a regiment found itself without a drum-major in 1875, the adjutant could always apply to Henry Potter & Co of 30 Charing Cross 'Makers to the Royal Family, War Office, India Office, Brigade of Guards, Army, Navy, Militia and Volunteer Corps etc'. Their illustrated catalogue of Military Band Instruments and Appurtenances carried the notice:

DRUM MAJORS

Commanding Officers requiring Drum or Bugle Majors can be accommodated with a list of men available for the position on application to H Potter & Co.

Beside drums, Henry Potter supplied 'Military Flutes (for Corps of Drums and Flutes)' and 'The Great Highland or Military Bagpipes of Cocus Wood, mounted in ivory £8 8s, mounted in silver £16 16s.' A flute cost £1 10s; drummers' aprons 'Polland Kharki, very light for India' 12s, deer skin £4 4s. Leopard skins could be supplied from six to 14 guineas, and Tiger Skins at 20 guineas.

It would seem that in 1876 the *Army & Navy Gazette* had wrongly credited Henry Potter & Co with the manufacture of a couple of silver kettledrums for the 5th Royal Irish Lancers, and on April 29 of that year a note appeared in another journal *Broad Arrow:*

5th LANCERS – Messrs GEORGE POTTER & CO of Aldershot should not be deprived of the credit of having manufactured the beautiful Silver Kettle Drums recently presented to the 5th Lancers, nor should Aldershot be supposed unequal to the task of producing such instruments. We have been requested to correct an error of the *Army & Navy Gazette* **on this point.**

In their own catalogue George Potter & Co stated that these kettledrums had been made to the order of Lieutenant Colonel Massey, honourable distinguished as 'Redan Massey', to replace those destroyed in the recent fire at the Tower of London. It took their craftsmen five months to hammer them out of sterling sheet silver weighing 960 ounces, and decorate them with the regimental devices of harp and crown and the motto 'Quis separabit?' in high relief supplemented by crossed lances. The names of various officers including the Duke of Montrose were engraved on both instruments.

'Kettledrummer of the Life Guards' by Alfred Munnings.
Reproduced courtesy of the Commanding Officer,
Household Cavalry Regiment.

Sidney Harris

'Rolling In' ceremony in The Royal Welch Fusiliers officers' mess on St David's Day.
Courtesy of Royal Welch Fusiliers Regimental Museum and Pitkin Pictorials Ltd.

1814

1915

1940

Silver drums may possibly be looked upon at first sight as an ornament of parade rather than an article of utility for musical purposes. But this is not quite the truth, as it is well known that the 'ring' of silver has a peculiar quality in relation to sound which renders it particularly available in many cases . . . In the present instance its superiority over the usual material employed is evident from the tone produced, which is both sweet and sonorous.

They believed that only four British regiments possessed silver kettle drums at that date, the 1st and 2nd Life Guards, the Royal Horse Guards (Blue) (which were the gift of royalty) and the 3rd Hussars who had been thought to have captured them from the French at the Battle of Dettingen, though the *Broad Arrow* had recently ascertained that it was the 7th Dragoon Guards who were responsible.

In their 1885 catalogue George Potter & Co offered not only brass and aluminium 14¾" diameter Side Drums Military Narrow or Cheese Pattern and Side Deep or Guards' Pattern, but also Tenor Drums 'introduced during the last century to replace the Kettle Drum'. They claimed to be the first people in Europe to manufacture aluminium kettledrums, as well as in silver and copper. They also made aluminium bass drums, a third the weight of brass, but called attention to their oak bass drums 'for hot and humid climates in preference to those supplied by inferior makers (sometimes in brass) which are heavy, clumsy and soon fall to pieces'. Their service included remodelling Russian and Foreign Trophy Drums; making Sterling Silver Side Drums for Presentation; and carrying out Painting and Heraldry 'by their skilled artist with as little delay as possible in accordance with General Order 41, Army Organisation, 11th April 1881'.

The Ground work of Cavalry Drums matches the colour of the tunic collar, excepting as in some Hussar Regiments where the collar is the same colour as the tunic, then it would match the Busby Bag. The Buffs (East Kent Regiment) still retain their old facings.

George Potter invented 'a marvellous system of instantaneously tuning kettledrums' and he demonstrated it in an exhibition in Manchester. He took out Royal Letters Patent and reckoned it would revolutionise the old system. Half a turn of a handle brought the drum in a moment from slack to highest pitch which was registered on an indicator.

Until this patent system of instantaneously tuning by sight is actually seen, naturally a heavy demand is made upon one's credulity, but when seen its simplicity and effect make it appear simply magical.

George Potter made Drum Majors' Staffs of superior malacca cane selected by the renowned native Hajji Ibrahim (?), with either a silver, silver plated or gilt metal head ornamented with the regimental devices in prices ranging from £4 to £50. They supplied drummers' aprons, drum-majors' dress sashes and kettledrum banners. They offered a whole page of Rules and Suggestions for the better management of drums on the strength of feeling such that their percussion instruments were 'by this time so universally known and appreciated as to entitle them to the credit so readily awarded by the public of their being the most celebrated Drum Makers in the World'.

Chapter 6

6   We're going, sir, ain't we?

Jakin and Lew, drummer boys of the Fore and the Aft in India; the Drum-Major's Manual of 1887; The Lincolnshires at Omdurman; the Boer War; the Great War; Swansong of The Drums?; Showpiece role? Drums and Bands; Corps of Drums Society; Rod-tensioning not for workshops; George Potter as 'emblazoners'.

Potter's customers were not only the regular regiments but the voluntary units which supplemented them, like the Arundel and Bramber Yeomanry Cavalry who spent summer evenings on the South Downs practising 'movements' and held an annual review watched by admiring wives and almost the entire local community in festive mood. The young gents demonstrated their accuracy with the pistol, and ability to thrust a sword through a ring, in competitions which brought the winners great glory. They broke off half way through for well-earned refreshment at The Maltsters Arms and in the evening dined riotously in the mess. Colourful uniforms, flags and booming music were essential ingredients of the yeomanry review, along with the beating of highly decorated drums with whitened ropes no longer functional but extremely ornamental.

It was good business for the suppliers of military musical instruments who had now increased in numbers not only in London but in Edinburgh and elsewhere. Whereas the Post Office London Directory of 1842 listed only Henry Potter, Cornelius Ward 'patentee of the newly invented drums [?]' and John Kohler, the 1870 edition gave seven drum manufacturers in addition to Henry Potter and including a competitor ten doors down, Rudall, Rose Carte & Co.

Drums were gradually becoming more and more ceremonial. Beating the Tattoo which, as seen, set the watch and warned innkeepers to turn off their taps, was evolving into a ceremony. The British Army made their own version of the custom of the devout and superstitious peasants of the armies of Imperial Russia who would sing a hymn before settling down for the night giving thanks for another day. The British took this and tied it to the Tattoo or Retreat which developed into an evening musical celebration, the beginnings of the Torchlight Tattoo and Tournament which was pure spectacle. There was now much military ceremony for ceremony's sake like the Field Day described by Charles Dickens in *Pickwick Papers* in which Drums and Fifes and the military band played a prominent part.

> **All looked at the sally-port and saw the colours fluttering gaily in the air, arms glistened brightly in the sun; column after column poured into the plain . . . The military bands struck up together; the horses stood upon two legs each, cantered backwards and whisked their tails about in all directions; the dogs barked, the mob screamed, the troops recovered.**

The Real Thing of course was somewhat different. But Drummer Stagpoole knew what was expected of him when he went with the 57th to New Zealand in 1860 and they had to attack the Maori stockades. He was awarded the Distinguished Conduct Medal and the Victoria Cross on two separate occasions in one week.

What must have made actual campaigning comfortingly familiar was the presence of the band and The Drums, even in the most remote theatres of war. A mounted band of 34 musicians accompanied The Inniskillings to Zululand in 1884, and found time to sit for their photograph in full dress scarlet tunics, blue overalls and pillbox caps. The tunic of the kettledrummer sitting astride his horse had a yellow collar, cuffs and shoulder strap. His kettledrums were draped with blue velvet banners with deep gold edging and a fringe. Embroidered on them in silver was the outline of the Castle of Inniskilling and above it the imperial crown. Three battle honours, Waterloo, Balaclava and Sevas-topol were inscribed on scrolls. The dark drum horse wore white stockings on its hind legs, and had a black sheepskin saddle cover with red edging.

The band and The Drums were with the 'Fore and Fit' regiment on the Afghan northwest frontier of India in the 1880s, the fictional adventures of which Rudyard Kipling described in his short story *Drums of the Fore and Aft*. It was based presumably on the actual activities of the 28th Foot who earned the name Fore and Aft when they were granted the unique privilege of wearing the regimental number 28 both on the back and the front of their hats after the rear rank had to stand with their backs to their comrades to repel French dragoons at the Battle of Alexandria in March 1801. In 1881 the 28th combined with the 61st as the 1st and 2nd Battalions, The Gloucestershire Regiment.

(93)
vance of an equal length of ſtep, and an equal cadence
or time of march.*

MUSIC AND DRUMS.

The uſe of muſic or drums, to *regulate* the march
in movement of manœuvre, is abſolutely forbid, as incompatible with the juſt and combined movements of
any conſiderable body, and *giving a falſe aid to the very
ſmalleſt.* They never perſevere in *ordered time,* or in
any other,—are conſtantly changing meaſure,—create
noiſe,—derange the equality of ſtep,—and counteract
the very end they are ſuppoſed to promote. The *ordered and cadenced march* can be acquired and preſer-
ved from the eye and habit alone, and troops muſt, by
great practice, be *ſo ſteadied* as to be able to maintain
it, even though drums or muſic of any kind ſhould
mark a different time.

* It was a conviction of the utility of the cadenced march, that
made the great Marſhal Saxe ſay, in his Reveries, " *That all the
myſteries of the Tactics were to be found in the legs."*

From **Instructions for the Drill,** *1803.*

Jakin and Lew were 'a brace of the most finished little fiends that ever banged
drum or tootled fife in the Band of a British regiment'. They had sprung from
the London gutter and joined the Fore and Fit when they were twelve. Two years
later they were with 900 others in barracks in India, members of a regiment
composed of drafts from one of Britain's over-populated manufacturing districts,
which had been 'put by' for many years and had no knowledge of what war meant.

Jakin and 'Piggy' Lew were bold, bad drummer boys who swore and drank,
and were always being birched by the Drum-Major for fighting or smoking. They
were hated by the other drummer boys. The Colonel told the Bandmaster to keep
The Drums in better discipline, and the Bandmaster said if they fought each
other again he would tell the Drum-Major to take the skin off their backs. Lew
had aspirations to be a 'musician'—he was the fifer and Jakin the drum beater.
When one of the trumpeters had to go to hospital, Lew volunteered to take his
place. He told the Bandmaster he wanted to learn to play every instrument in the
band, and the Bandmaster told him there was nothing to stop him being a
Bandmaster one day.

'Said you might be a bloomin' non-combatant, did 'e?' said Jakin. 'That's just
about wot 'e would say. I've put in my boy's service; it's a bloomin' shame that
doesn't count for pension—I'll take on as a privit. Then I'll be a Lance in a year.
In three years I'll be a bloomin' sergeant.' He would finally become an officer
and ask Bandmaster Lew to have a glass of sherry wine in the ante-room.

Jakin and Lew were badly shaken when they heard the regiment was to go on active service against the 'Paythans'—the War of the Lost Tribes. What would happen to The Drums? Would the Band go to the front? How many of The Drums would go with them if they did?

Jakin thought it more likely that The Drums would be left behind at the depot with the women. He wished he was a bugler like Tom Kidd. If the two of them held Tom and kicked him so hard he could no longer blow a bugle, then maybe Jakin could go in his place? But then perhaps the weak hearts, which all that smoking had given them, would make them medically unfit? When the two of them see the colonel coming, Jakin accosts him.

'We're going sir, ain't we?'

'You? You'd die in the first march!'

But surely, said Jakin, if Tom Kidd, who had very-close veins, was going, they could? Well, said the Colonel, the Band was certainly going, and if they were passed by the doctor daresay they could go with it.

Public feeling among the drummer boys rose to fever pitch and the lives of Jakin and Lew became unenviable. Not only had they been permitted to enlist two years before the regulation boy's age—fourteen—but by virtue it seemed of their extreme youth they were now allowed to go to the Front, which thing had not happened to acting-drummers within the knowledge of boy. The Band which was to accompany the Regiment had been cut down to the regulation twenty men, the surplus returning to the ranks. Jakin and Lew were attached to the Band as supernumeraries, though they would much have preferred being Company buglers.

The Brigadier's plan was for three regiments to debouch from three gorges and annihilate the Afghans in the fourth. The Fore and Fit were led down their gorge by their band which, on reaching open ground, wheeled to the right 'and retired behind a little rocky knoll, still playing while the regiment went past'. They heard bugles bringing the Ghurkas forward at the double, and Highland pipes on their left. When 300 six foot drug-crazed Ghazi fiends bore down on them brandishing knives eight feet long, they turned and fled back into the narrow pass from which they had just emerged. The Band fled too, leaving their instruments behind them on the knoll. Jakin and Lew's short legs soon left them 50 yards behind, and they decided it would be safer to return to the rock where they hoped the Afghans would not see them.

'They've gone and left us alone here!' wailed Jakin. 'Wot'll we do? We're all that's left of the band and we'll be cut up as sure as death.'

'I'll die game then' said Lew fumbling with his tiny drummer's sword.

They both took a swig of rum from the water bottles left behind by the bandsmen—and that gave Jakin an idea.

'Tip our bloomin' cowards yonder the word to come back. Come on Lew, we won't get 'urt. Take the fife and give me the drum. The Old Step for all your blooming gut's worth!'

> He slipped the drum-sling over his shoulder, thrust the fife into Lew's hand, and the two boys marched out of the cover of the rock into the open making a hideous hash of the first bars of *The British Grenadiers.* A few of the Fore and Fit had already started to come back in response to their officers' abuse, but the tune settled into full swing and the boys kept shoulder to shoulder Jakin banging the drum as one possessed. The one fife made a thin and pitiful squeaking but the tune carried far, even to the Ghurkas.

Jakin halted and beat the long roll of the Assembly, while Lew's fife squealed despairingly. They then wheeled and marched back. The Fore and Fit, their spirit restored by the boys' heroic gesture, poured out into the valley. The Afghans were told not to kill the British drummer boys but take them alive and convert them to their faith,

> but the first volley had been fired and Lew dropped on his face. Jakin stood for a minute, spun round and collapsed as the Fore and Fit came forward, the curses of their officers in their ears and in their hearts the shame of open shame. Half the men had seen the drummers die, and they made no sign. They did not even shout. They doubled out straight across the plain in open order, and they did not fire.

Jakin and Lew, or whatever their real names were, never lived to pursue their musical careers, or else they would have been given to study *The Drum-Major's Manual* which Henry Potter & Co brought out in 1887 as a very heavily revised version of Samuel Potter's *The Art of Beating The Drum* of 1810. He probably would not have been able to make head or tails of it, but Jakin would surely have approved of the observation:

> To make a good side-drummer it is of the utmost importance that the training should take place during boyhood whilst the muscles of the wrist are supple.

If started later, when muscles were set, it was doubtful if side-drum beating worthy of the name could ever be accomplished.

THE FUNERAL OF A CAPTAIN
IN THE ARMY

On the march a drummer carried the bass drum in front of him. The large headed stick for the right hand was used principally to mark the time, and the small one in the left hand for intermediate accompaniment. 'But this accompaniment must not degenerate into an injudicious monotony; the primary object of bass drum beating being to keep *strict* marching time for the regiment.' The bass drummer should not only be a good timist but incapable of being led away by any melody detrimental to regulation time. In most regiments it was customary for bass drummers to flourish the drum sticks somewhat briskly between the occasional beats when marching. As that spirit of beating was still observed, though not to so great an extent as formerly, it must be left to the discretion of the bass drummer himself as to the effects produced on this style of using his drum sticks.

Kettledrums, stated the manual, were for cavalry in pairs, one bigger than the other, tuned to sound the tonic and dominant note of the key in which the music is written by handles round the side. Kettledrummers were advised not to overstrain the vellum. Low notes were more resonant and heard at a greater distance than high notes. Each kettledrum had a compass of about four notes, the large one from G to D and the small one from C to F.

The most important qualifications for cavalry drumming are To tune the drum correctly; To keep exact time; and To possess the necessary assurance to use the sticks with freedom, and To present an attractive figure at the head of the regiment.

Henry Potter reminded his readers that Handel scored the *Te Deum* he wrote to celebrate the victorious battle of Dettingen for two kettledrums, and the instruments played on were those captured from the French at that engagement. What he did not mention, perhaps because he did not know, was that Alexander Pope immortalised the occasion in Book IV of *The Dunciad:*

> **Strong in new Arms, lo! Giant HANDEL stands,**
> **Like bold Briareus, with a hundred hands;**
> **To stir, to rouse, to shake the soul he comes,**
> **And Jove's own Thunders follow Mars's Drums.**

In this manual a hundred years ago Henry Potter used the phrase 'Corps of Drums and Flutes'—the first time The Drums were called a corps? 'Flute' was now preferred to 'Fife' fairly universally. He had a section 'Drum and Flute Duty' which included a list of Calls for Camp, Quarters and in the Field. There was Defaulters (The Taps); Guard Salute; Pioneers Fatigue; Picquet; Men's Breakfast and Tea; Men's Dinner ('Roast Beef of Old England'); Rations ('Hearts of Oak'); School ('Sailor Jack'); Recruiting and Church; the Salute (or Point of War); The Funeral March ('Dead March in Saul').

His recommended composition of a Corps of Drums and Flutes was two piccolos, two F flutes, four 1st flutes, two 2nd flutes, two 3rd flutes, 1 leading drummer, five side drums, one triangle and one bass drum. They would march separately from the band which would precede it.

But this was the stuff of the depot—designed privately as the camp time-keeper and publicly to impress would-be recruits, which it did very effectively. But those who, at the end of Queen Victoria's reign, enlisted in Her Majesty's forces to help enlarge her empire and found themselves in foreign parts not yet coloured red, came to value The Drums in a different currency as the morale raiser on the march which had been their raison d'etre from their first military use in the days of the Tudors.

Lieutenant Hamilton Hodgson was to appreciate their worth in this respect when he was sent with The Lincolnshires as part of General Kitchener's army dispatched to occupy Sudan and eventually invade and conquer Egypt. On their way south beside the Nile they had several skirmishes with the Sudanese but there was a full-scale battle on September 2, 1898 at Omdurman outside Khartoum. Five days before the clash with the dervishes, 11,000 of whom were killed, The Lincolnshires were slogging their way in the heat over terrain that was very different from the levelled parade ground of the depot at home. On August 26 1898, Hodgson wrote in his diary:

> **The whole division paraded, and that, combined with the fact**
> **that the going was very bad—rising ground with loose stones**
> **and constantly passing dry water courses with tussocks of**
> **rough grass and stunted mimosa and other thorny bushes—**
> **made the march very trying and tiring . . . After the third halt**

made the march very trying and tiring . . . After the third halt
someone shouted out it was all down hill the rest of the way
which was cheering, and The Drums came across some better
ground and started playing; and in fact played us into camp.
I don't think I ever appreciated drums more. They got a
very long step, and soon the whole brigade were going to the
step. After each time they were applauded and cheered
vociferously. Drummer Hill, our show drummer who prides
himself on having a black mark the size of a penny on the
centre of the vellum, got his chance occasionally with a side
drum solo. Poor chap, his drumming days are over as he is
wounded in his writs – bullet came through drum first.

And on the day of the battle, September 2, The Drums were in there too.

Soudanese Brigade playing at bugles—the 10th playing "The
Poachers". About half an hour later they had been blocked
and halted, and we passed them, our drums playing. They
gave us a captured standard to carry ahead; more howls.

The Drums were in the firing line in the war in South Africa too, where the
heat was equally unbearable, and had many casualties. Private E C Moffet described
what happened when he was with the 2nd Battalion The Scots Guard (1,000 men
in eight companies) at the Battle of Biddulphsburg in 1900 and they were ordered
to capture a Boer gun:

Scarcely had the order been given for the Grenadiers to
advance when shells in quick succession came from the Boer
gun above the farm; this appeared to be the signal for the
enemy's rifle to commence, and our first casualty was
Drummer Clark, shot through the wrist. . . . During the height
of the action Colonel Lloyd [the CO] was badly wounded and
was gallantly attended by Drummer Haines who, while in the
act of supporting his colonel, was also himself badly wounded.

Drummer Haines in fact saved his commanding officer's life by pulling him to
the shelter of an ant heap.
Drummer William Barton of the 2nd Battalion Royal Irish Fusiliers who moved
from Colchester to South Africa in October 1899 also kept a diary (now in the
Public Record Office, Northern Ireland) but in it he had nothing to say about his
activities in The Drums or the exploits of fellow drummers.
The going was so hard for The Buffs in February 1900 advacing on Bloemfontein
that one Mick Brophy took Boy Harry Carter's drum and threw it into the river.

'My heart bled' he said, 'to see a tiny whipper snapper of a young lad of 16 carrying a full marching order and a drum for miles across the African veldt.'

When they captured and entered Bloemfontein there were only 12 drummers left to lead them in triumph. Drumheads got broken; flutes filled with sand. When the regiment first went to South Africa in December 1889 they sent their painted side-drums to the depot at Canterbury for safe keeping. They took the seven 'Government' side-drums to the war, plus a painted bass drum. In 1903 they had their Government drums replaced by Ordnance and got George Potter of Aldershot to paint them. Their 'private' drums were re-blocked and renovated. Thus by 1904 16 painted side-drums and two bass drums were in good order, and they all returned to South Africa with the battalion in 1905. In 1907 they added a tenor drum—their first.

For some the beating of a drum had less than triumphal associations—for instance A E Housman who in *A Shropshire Lad*, published in 1896, wrote:

> *On the idle hill of summer*
> *Sleepy with the flow of streams,*
> *Far I hear the steady drummer*
> *Drumming like a noise in dreams.*

> *Far and near and low and louder*
> *On the roads of earth go by,*
> *Dear to friends and food for powder,*
> *Soldiers marching, all to die.*

> *Far the calling bugles hollo,*
> *High the screaming fife replies,*
> *Gay the files of scarlet follow:*
> *Woman bore me, I will rise.*

But the days of campaigning in scarlet were numbered. The dust-coloured uniform worn by British and native troops in India from the middle of the nineteenth century, and known as khaki, was adopted as camouflage in the South African War and soon became universal. Warfare was becoming less of a pageant. The Drummer's Sword with its 19 inch blade introduced in 1857 was dropped in 1903 as obsolete. With the regiments home again however and peacetime routines re-assumed, the Sergeant-Drummer, as Drum-Majors were now called, still managed to be the most colourful man on parade.

In 1906 Sergeant-Drummers of the line were clothed as Staff-Sergeants with gold-laced wings to their tunics. They continued to wear drum-belts on which the battle honours of the regiment and any special regimental badges or distinctions were embroidered, in addition to the regulation Royal Cypher and Crown and miniature drum sticks—to remind them of the days when they actually were side-drum beaters. They wore white gauntlets instead of gloves. On ordinary occasions Sergeant-Drummers of the Foot Guards wore a richly laced tunic similar to the bandsmen but more ornate. On State occasions they wore a coat of ruby velvet nearly covered with gold lace and embroidery. They had a richly embroidered Royal Cypher and Crown on the breast identical to the coats worn by the bandsmen and trumpeters of the Household Cavalry. Round the waist was a crimson sash with a heavy gold fringe held in place by a regimental brooch; on their legs dark blue knee breeches and long red cloth leggings and gold lace garters; on their head a jockey cap of royal blue. In winter a ruby red cloak with dark blue velvet collar trimmed with gold lace was worn. The staff both winter and summer was decorated with gold acorns just above the ferrule.

An article in *The Army and Navy Chronicle* carried a sketch of the Drum-Major of the Fighting Fifth (the Northumberland Fusiliers) in the full uniform of 1906. 'Like the Drum-Major of the Old Cameronians in 1852' states the writer,

> **the 5th Drum-Major wears the plume (in this case a white one tipped with red) coiling right over the top of the bearskin cap. It is perhaps worthy to note that in this regiment the Drum-Major carries, in the case of the 1st Battalion, a silver staff; and in the 2nd Battalion an ebony one, heavily mounted in silver, the ancient badge of the regiment, St George and the Dragon, surmounting the whole.**

The duties of the Sergeant-Drummer were much as they had always been, 'the supervision and instruction of the drummers and "boys" in the use of the drum, flute (erroneously termed "fife") and bugle, and is responsible for their regular practice and behaviour. He has to see that the orderly-buglers perform their duties in camp or barracks, and that the prescribed calls are properly sounded at the appointed hours. In additiion to these duties he is ex-officio postmaster to his battalion.' The day's mail would be deposited in the Sergeant-Drummer's office and he would be responsible for distributing it to the officers and Other Ranks, an extra job for which he was paid—which will have been very welcome.

> **As Alexander had no more worlds to conquer, so the Sargeant-Drummer like the Field-Marshal, is at the top of the military tree in his profession. He only receives however the pay of an ordinary sergeant viz. 2s 4d per diem; hence many drummers on arriving at a sufficient age for service in the ranks elect to adopt that course as offering a wider field for promotion than the "drums".**

It was also evident that The Drums had had their heyday and were slowly receding into history. In camp and in parade ground ceremonial they held their own, but what would be their role in another armed conflict whose nature would be totally different from any that had gone before, where there were no pitched battles, and talk of 'in the field' meant in the trenches or out in No Man's Land?

When Britain and her allies declared war against the Kaiser's Germany in 1914 and The Buffs were called home to mobilise, they placed all the instruments of their Corps of Drums into safe-keeping and went off to France. No more use for them? Within a few months they sent for eight side-drums and half a dozen flutes and formed a new Corps of Drums in France to carry out the earliest of functions, putting heart into weary soldiers on the march, giving their lungs a rest from non-stop singing. Not only that. At the Battle of Loos in September 1915 the drummers of The Buffs took their place beside their comrades as riflemen in the ranks. There were heavy casualties and only a few drummers survived. But a Corps of Drums was gradually built up once more and accompanied the battalion throughout the rest of the war including the campaigns in Salonika and at Constantinople.

Fear of having his drum captured by the enemy, which had haunted his predecessors for 300 years, so worried Drummer Smith of the 1st Battalion The Bedfordshire Regiment (which with The Hertfordshire and Essex Regiments was to form The Royal Anglian Regiment) that during the retreat from Mons in 1914 he left it at a Belgian farm called La Paturage. Madame Chancine, the farmer's wife, disguised the drum as a hat box throughout the Germans' occupation of the town and they never rumbled it. In January 1919 Brigadier General H C Jackson recovered Drummer Smith's side-drum and gave Madame a replica. In the depot the original drum was honoured with a special sling and silver badge inscribed 'Mons'.

Brigadier General James Jack, who went from the Cameronians to command the 2nd West Yorks, re-formed their Drums as a priority and had them playing on the march, beating Retreat when the battalion was out of the line, and playing for Mess dinner nights. When not drumming, the drummers filled many functions of which the most normal and dangerous was that of stretcher bearer.

When, at the time of the Retreat from Mons, Major Bridges came across 400 dead tired, hungry, dirty stragglers wandering round St Quentin, he went into a toy shop and bought a tin whistle and a toy drum. He gave the whistle to his trumpeter, told him to march off playing well known tunes such as *Tipperary* and *The British Grenadiers*, and then followed him 'beating the drum like mad'. The stragglers gaped and laughed at first, but then one by one they formed up and were soon marching to the beat of the toy drum and penny whistle to rejoin their regiments. The incident inspired another poem about a drum from Sir Henry Newbolt, *The Toy Band, a Song of the Great Retreat.*

His earlier verses, as every schoolboy knows, had been about the drum of Sir Francis Drake who served as a Vice-Admiral in the *Revenge* in the battle against the Spanish Armada exactly four hundred years ago in 1588.

'Take my drum to England, hang it by the shore,
Strike it when your powder's running low;
If the Dons sight Devon, I'll quit the port o' Heaven,
An' drum them up the Channel as we drummed them long ago.

The spirits – if not the powder – of those demoralised stragglers from their regiments at the Retreat from Mons were certainly running extremely low, but they were magically raised by the drum and fife from St Quentin's toy shop. A more earthy and entirely new use for drum beats was made in 1915 to train men of the 3rd Battalion Grenadier Guards to follow the secret weapons which, to hide their true nature, the British called 'tanks'. To discipline troops into keeping 50 yards behind a creeping barrage of firing tanks, without there having been a preliminary bombardment, there were rehearsals behind the lines with drum beats representing the firing of the tanks' guns. If any German spy had heard these strange goings-on, he would have dismissed them as just another practice of the Corps of Drums. So the element of surprise was well maintained when, on September 15 1916, the Guards Division on the Somme attacked in front of Ginchy with these science-fiction tracked vehicles rolling forward on their tracks. The 3rd Battalion Grenadier Guards advanced with four platoons forward and four in support. It was the first battle in which 'tanks' had been employed. The battalion fought their way through, with 18 out of their 21 officers killed, including Raymond Asquith. But the tanks ahead of them soon lost direction or broke down.

Out of the line The Drums helped to take the mind off 'the prolonged drudgery with fearful moments' of life up at the front. At Bethune on St Davids Day March 1 1916 The Drums of The Royal Welch Fusiliers played *Old Mother Riley,* and after Salute marched round the barrack square and through the streets where the officers were billeted to the air of *The Staffordshire Knot.* A leek was given to each man, and The Drums gilded the leeks given to the officers.

In his diary of those years, Captain C J Dunn of The Royal Welch Fusiliers, calling himself 'One Of Their Medical Officers', bore witness to The Drums' final years of active service – the swansong of the military drum? When in January 1917 their division was going up to relieve the French 17th Division in the Clery sector, marching at two o'clock in the afternoon on well-repaired roads, the R W F passed French artillery pulling out. 'They were mightily interested in our Drums' noted Dunn. When in the previous autumn the Prince of Wales came over from Corps HQ to visit the battalion at Méaulte, he was informally received in the mess 'after listening to The Drums'.

On Christmas Day 1917 at Poperinghe, the Signals and Runners subscribed for a dinner of their own, and so did The Drums. 'Major Kearsley and Captain Radford had to drink the Signals' cocktail, a tumbleful of beer and sweet champagne; they jibbed at The Drums' neat whisky and were given "porto".' In April 1918 the battalion started marching from Villers-Bocage at midday, and because the head of column took a wrong turning and added three and a half miles to the route, they did not arrive at Hédauville until eight that evening.

The day was hot and the march trying; the men got fed up with being told "It's only one kilometre more". They ached with every weary pace; sore feet that had not been washed for a week or more, and fatigue, caused 60 to fall out. The Drums played wonderfully, since last night Hedges burst the big drum. "What's the use of worrying?" always met with some response. We got into Hédauville at 8 pm very tired; billets filthy. New unwashed socks are not the best to march in.

It was nearing the end of the ordeal when in April 1918 the battalion moved out of Hérissart at half past five in the morning. 'When we passed The Drums they played *Goodbye-ee!* which some thought in bad taste.' It was completely over when in November 1918 the Prince of Wales visited The Royal Welch Fusiliers Officers' Mess once again. After lunch he toured the battalion 'to have a look at the men' and particularly those with medal ribbons. He had a long talk with the grey-haired, perky, quarrelsome little Sergeant-Drummer Dyer who had been awarded the M S M. His Royal Highness recalled having seen Dyer on a previous visit to the battalion, and 'Dyer gave him chapter and verse waxing loquacious and bursting with pride.'

On February 17 The Drums were joined by the Regimental Band.

'Brave Drummer Boy'

It was a symbolic move. As the military band grew in size and importance, the Corps of Drums shrunk. In English line regiments it gradually fell into disuse. Many retained them as showpieces but after 1918 their function had gone. With the cut-backs in the Army after the Great War there were neither the funds nor the personnel for fringe activities such as maintaining a Corps of Drums. But more than anything else the run down of The Drums was due to the fact that the Army had begun to stop marching and taken to motor transport. There has been no change in drummers' uniform; 1914 is standard year.

With the fighting over and ending in victory for the Allies, the combination of Regimental Band and such Corps of Drums as continued to exist, became more prominent – though of course each was still separate and a law unto themselves. The Buffs returned to Dover in April 1919 and when in October they embarked for India The Drums of the battalion played them down the hill from Dover Castle to board ship. In the Punjab Band and Drums were quartered together. Though the battalion was on a war footing, Band and Drums accompanied it to Mesopotamia, where however there were no roads so no marching to the drum. The Corps of Drums which went with The Buffs to Aden in 1922 however consisted of 40 men. They proudly took part in the Aldershot Torchlight Tattoo in 1926, and even more proudly marched through the City of London in July 1928 with drums beating and colours flying after receiving new colours from the Lord Mayor. Two years later the battalion was presented with a new set of drums. They at least were in no hurry to get shot of a time-honourd tradition.

> **The men may change,**
> **Their clothing alter,**
> **Old drums may be replaced by new,**
> **But the spirit of the drum has remained unvaried**
> **Since May Day Fifteen Seventy Two.**

Though regiments began to dispense with their Corps of Drums, they still had drummers in their regimental bands. A military band of bandsmen playing 'music' (soldiers, as seen, since 1803) sitting in a bandstand had their own kettle drummers and bass drummers who were not of course members of the Corps of Drums and were not in fact known as drummers but 'percussionists'. They wore a Musician's Badge not a Drummer's. In the Grenadier Guards the bass drummer was known as a Time-Beater. When the band was marching, the players of oboes and other reed instruments which it was impossible to play on the move without choking, augmented the regular percussionists who played side-drums, a bass drum and cymbals. If the Corps of Drums was taking part in the same parade, they marched separately from the band, remaining silent while the band played, and vice versa.

Corps of Drums *and Pipes* (bagpipes) were never dropped by the Scottish regiments in spite of their also starting to drive about in motor vehicles. With so magnificent an appearance, they were considered a great aid to recruiting.

Scotsmen incidentally held their side-drums vertical at their knee, while Englishmen carried them tipped at an angle.

In England, The Buffs having just received their new drums, were so confident in the continuing role of the military drum that in 1931 the 2nd Battalion issued a *Manual for the Drums*. Stated the Introduction:

> **The effect of The Drums is to instil into the soldier the swing and the movement of marching as opposed to the action of walking ... Not only is the music of the Drums a wonderful aid to troops on the march but it is also an aid to a soldier's carriage and the morale for which the British Infantryman is so justly famous.**

The composition of a Corps of Drums should be: 1 leading side-drummer and seven side-drummers; 4 tenor drummers; 1 bass drummer; triangle; cymbals; 13 flutes; 2 piccolos and a bass flute. All drummers should be able to play the bugle and beat a bass drum. When marching for parade duties and ceremonial as much swagger as possible should be put into all movements. Playing the battalion on parade the Corps should play *Wha wouldna' fecht for Charlie*. For Calling the Roll the parade drummer should beat *Orderly Sergeants;* for Receiving the Lieutenant Colonel on Parade, *Attention for the Lieutenant Colonel*. For Church Parade the *Long Dress for Parade* should be sounded when the CO was there in person. For Reveille drummers must beat *Point of War* and then *The Mother and Three Camps* (Old Mother Jenkins). At Church Parade while the battalion was being inspected the band and The Drums should march up and down playing *Hark the bonny Christchurch bells!* and a hymn; then march and counter march on *The Church Call*.

The enthusiasm with which The Buffs encouraged their Corps of Drums was shared by many others. At the Tidworth and Aldershot Tattoos in the 1930s there would be more than 30 of them with an average of 36 players in each battalion. But the spectacular mock battles and displays of the Torchlight Tattoos were soon to be displaced by scenes of greater realism.

Presentation of drums to 43rd Regiment 1847

When the Second World War broke out in 1939 bandsmen became stretcher bearers and drummers joined an Anti-Aircraft Platoon, an Intelligence Section or a Carrier Platoon. Many became the Defence Platoon. But Corps of Drums as such were mostly broken up. In 1984 one-time Drum-Major C Gay of the 1st Battalion The Worcestershire Regiment recollected how in 1940 out of the 26 members of The Drums which went to Palestine in 1938 he was the only one left, a Lance Sergeant.

But for many units of the British Expeditionary Force which landed in France in 1939 the Drum was still the ark of the covenant symbolising the soul of the regiment as it had been when to hear the colonel's drummer beating gave men in the line the audible assurance that the colours were safe. Rather than risk their drums being captured when the Highland Division was about to be overrun at St Valery in 1940, they buried them in the hope of recovering them later – which they did in 1945. Similarly in the retreat to Dunkirk the 2nd Battalion The Worcestershire Regiment made sure their drums never fell into the hands of the Germans by burying them. Only two of them were returned to them after the war, one from Denmark.

The war produced its ceremonial occcasion too, as when in June 1943 The Irish Brigade made a formal visit to the Pope in Rome and a representative party of 150 marched behind their Pipes and Drums up the steps of the Vatican. His Holiness was received by three pipe majors playing *The Minstrel Boy*. After a special Mass in St Peter's the Pipes and Drums beat Retreat in the piazza outside the basilica.

Drum-Major Gay who had been a Prisoner of War rejoined his battalion in Cairo in 1945 where he found all the drums and flutes had been handed in to the 'Auditors' in 1941. He formed a new Corps of Drums and after three months of practising held their first RSM's Parade. But The Drums were forgotten when the battalion, now mostly National Service men, went to Malaya. In Jamaica however where the unit was mainly regulars again, a new Corps of Drums was formed reporting to the Adjutant. But he saw little chance of ever returning to the circumstances of Before The War when every drummer could read music and write basic music.

> **To have a good Corps of Drums, all the drummers must be able to read music. No NCO should be unable to read music. Drum Majors should be able to play a flute as well as a side-drum, and the Drums must practise and practise. I have known a flute-player start practising in a barrack room, and within a short time the whole Corps of Drums would be blowing and beating away. (*Drummers Call* no 24, Spring 1984)**

Since 1945, formation of a Corps of Drums in line units of the British Army has been optional at the discretion of the Commanding Officer. Where the decision has been taken to carry on the tradition, there have been many heartening stories of men who have been inspired by it to make it their vocation. Such a one was Drum-Major Lively who joined The Buffs as a boy drummer in September 1958. Posted to the 1st Battalion The Queen's Own Buffs, he joined their Corps of Drums in 1961. He was promoted Drum-Sergeant in September 1966 and appointed Drum-Major of the 2nd Battalion The Queen's Regiment in April 1967. In the Birthday Honours of 1970 he received the British Empire Medal.

But then the situation deteriorated, and to arrest the process several enthusiasts, including Roger Davenport, in 1977 formed The Corps of Drums Society to discover where active drum and flute corps existed and make a list of them. As they stated later, they considered 'the drum and flute corps that our fathers knew is, if not exactly dead, then in a state of advanced decrepitude'.

In the first issue of their newsletter *The Drummers Call* of April 1978, the leading article deplored the fact that

> To-day it is not even necessary for the routine barrack calls to be sounded (though this is still done in many battalions) and the Corps of Drums is entirely a ceremonial body whose primary task must be their allotted military function within the battalion. On a ceremonial parade however many Corps of Drums have become merely an extension of the regimental band and very rarely parade on their own . . . The Royal Military School of Music [Kneller Hall] have stated that they have no jurisdiction or authority over the training or establishment of drummers, fifers, buglers, trumpeters etc.

So the Corps of Drums Society hoped 'to preserve the Corps of Drums style of music as a living thing before it is too late'. To this end, at the instigation of (as he then was) WO2 (RQMS) Mike Hall and Major (QM) J A Barrow MBE of The Duke of Edinburgh's Royal Regiment (Berkshire and Wiltshire), the Ministry of Defence published as an Infantry Training manual in 1985 *The Drummer's Handbook* (Army Code 71333) with a Foreword by Major General C T Shortis, Director of Infantry, in which he stated:

> It was felt that with the more rapid turnover in personnel in Corps of Drums, particularly in the Infantry of the Line battalions, the customs, traditions and their music too, which had been passed on amongst the long serving drummers, would have become lost and distorted because so little had been put to print over the years.

The ceremonial splendour of the full dress parade had now lost its place in the battle of priorities for time and resources to the more earnest work of training for operations in the field. With it had gone much of the ingrained knowledge of how to perform as well as the standards at which to aim. The Handbook, therefore, set out to provide a common reference work on all Drums matters. It deals with full dress and accoutrements which in many regiments were showing unhappy and expensive signs of deviation from tradition. It provides detailed coverage of staff and parade cane drill for drum majors so that this was common when bands and drums were massed. Perhaps even more important for the future the Handbook offers sections on music theory and on techniques with drum, flute and bugle. The Handbook was a labour of love for Mike Hall and Jack Barrow, and its publication may yet be seen to have been as important for Drums as recognition by the Duke of Cambridge of the need for Kneller Hall was for military music.

In 1981 however all eight battalions of Foot Guards had strong Corps of Drums, as did the Guards Depot. They always marched behind the band; but Scots and Irish Guards parading without bands had the Drums and Pipes in front. At Beating the Retreat 1987 in which 220 men of the Massed Bands of the Guards Divisions took part, Drum-Major Dave Davidson of The Scots Guards led the Drums and Pipes. Senior Drum-Major Dixie Dean led the Massed Corps of Drums. It was his last Beating the Retreat. Respendent kettledrummers beat time for the Massed Mounted Bands of the Household Cavalry.

The Drummer's Handbook recommends a modern Corps of Drums should consist of a Drum Major and 16 drummers based on the eight company battalion of 1914, with five side-drums, one tenor drum, one bass drum, one cymbals, five first B flat flutes, two first F flat flutes, and one piccolo. It is a lot of men to train. But the real problem is that financial cuts have removed the drummers from the establishment and converted drumming into a hobby. That said, they are given an amount of equipment from official sources and an amount of basic drums training: in most Divisional Depots, some 20-26 weeks. But when he reaches his battalion, the young drummer earns his pay and, more keenly than at any time before, his promotion, more by his ability with rifle and machine gun than with drum and flute. There is no central training: hardly a system to produce uniformity of performance. By contrast, the Royal Marines train their drummers at one central depot, the Royal Marines School of Music at Deal. Attached to each Royal Marines Band is an instructor from Deal so that drumming throughout the Corps is admirably uniform. Roger Davenport of the Corps of Drums Society believes that the Infantry might do worse than take a leaf from the Royal Marines book, but the Army has yet to be convinced. In the meantime the Society is covering the gap. Army Cadet Forces are expected to introduce music into their training syllabus, the Drums option in line with guidance from the Corps of Drums Society. In short the spirit is very much alive and if the Society has anything to do with it, drumming in the British Army is again a rising star.

To whatever extent consistency can be hoped for within Britain, the drumming traditions of the British infantry could hardly be expected to have travelled across the Atlantic without suffering some degree of deviation. But doubtless it would be difficult to fault the performances of the 1st Michigan Colonial Fife and Drum Corps formed in 1974, whose repertoire includes calls such as *Three Camps* and *Reveille* and the marches *Bonnie Dundee, The Buff Coat* and *Ça Ira* played by The West Yorkshire Regiment at the Battle of Farmars in 1793. In the war in which they fought for their independence, the drummers of the rebel American colonists beat the same calls and played the same music as the British redcoats who stormed the redoubt at Bunker Hill, for they had inherited them from the same source. The people of New England and Old England, now foes, spoke and understood the same tongue – and that included the Language of The Drum.

In trying to reproduce eighteenth century music in the 1980s the drummers of Michigan beat the vellum, rope-tensioned drums of the period with their deep notes.

Many on both sides of the Atlantic and in other parts of the world deplored the replacement of the centuries-old rope-tensioned by the rod-tensioned drum, and one with a head of plastic instead of calfskin (and the best reputedly from 'Slunk Calfskin' belonging to a calf that was stillborn).

Stretched skin slackened when it got wet, and changed the drum's note. After continual wetting the drum head became soggy and unbeatable. A stick went through it like cardboard. Many experiments were carried out to find a way of making skin unaffected by rain, including varnishing and clipping on a thin plastic sheet, before settling for a wholly plastic head which gave a very much crisper tone. It was an unfortunate deviation which had to be measured against the benefit of being able to retain the pitch in a prolonged downpour. In spite of the unpopular hard, flat noise not being the 'real' drum sound, its advantages were obvious. But the Army were not to be rushed. They first introduced a 'Nylon' woven head, supposed to be weather-proof, in the early 1950s. But beating it for a long time in the rain beat the water into the fibres and the drum lost its tone. They substituted a plastic with a rougher surface and of a different weight which in the last three years has been replaced by a new head, brown in colour and of even coarser weave which is impervious to all kinds of weather.

How tightly the animal skin was stretched across the shell of a drum – the tension – was determined by ropes. In hot weather the drum head got tighter and the ropes slacker. Maintaining a rope-tensioned drum could be long and laborious. The drum looked good, but to clean it a drummer was supposed to strip it down, clean the shell with metal polish, re-assemble it, blanco the ropes and re-polish the shell where the white had rubbed off. However, as is their wont, soldiers found a way round this. They applied polish to the metal shell around and under the ropes and then shone it with a strip of old army blanket about five inches wide and three feet long. This was pulled back and forth with the hands while the drum was steadied with the feet. Then all the ropes and braces would be carefully blancoed.

But science was on the way and Cornelius Ward took out a patent for tightening a drum head more conveniently – by rods – in the early 1830s; indeed a type of rod-tensioned drum of 1805 can be seen in the Scottish United Services Museum to-day. But Ward's device ran into stress and strain problems and could only be applied to small drums. The British War Office rejected it – and went on rejecting any form of rod-tensioned drum with its higher tension and higher pitch until the 1950s – in spite of its use by military bands elsewhere in the world. The trouble was it did not *look* right and it was heavier, but above all it *broke with tradition*.

The officers of many Territorial Army bands, who were not restricted as regular regiments were, began buying rod-tensioned drums after World War 2. Some Light Infantry regiments followed suit; and in the mid-1960s the Brigade of Guards went over to them but still with a wooden hoop. Only gradually did the infantry reconcile themselves to having metal hoops; the Royal Marines did not do so until 1986, while the Guards have yet to do so except in pipe bands. The rod-tensioned, plastic head, military drum is now regulation issue throughout the British Army – and from now on anything else will be untraditional.

At the centre of this revolution were the people who had made drums for the armies of the Duke of Marlborough and the Duke of Wellington, the Potter family whose association had always been more with Corps of Drums than military bands. Major J G R Potter owned both the London business of Henry Potter & Co which had moved from Charing Cross Road to West Street in 1900 (and has since moved out of the West End altogether), and the Aldershot business of George Potter & Co in Bank Street. When he died in 1968 the major's private limited companies passed into the hands of Arthur Newell who became chairman. In 1985 David Leech, and two others who had already bought shares in the business, took it over. David Leech became chairman and managing director, and the other two working directors. Potters become 'management owned' – a single enterprise.

British infantry regiments ordered drums for their Corps of Drums from Ordnance who had them made with wooden shells plain unadorned and rod-tensioned with plastic heads, by Premier Percussion Ltd of Leicester whose managing director was Roger Horrobin. Regiments then sent the drums to George Potter & Co of Aldershot for 'emblazoning' – at their own expense. The work was carried out by the heraldic artist Christopher Collins who had done it for Potters exclusively since 1966. On the shell of the drum he painted the title of the battalion, the regiment's crest and battle honours. For the drums of the Guards Division he had to put the Royal Arms upon a stand of the Queen's and Regimental Colours surmounted by the regimental ribbon on a very dark blue ground. The Commanding Officer of each regiment of the line decided what heraldry was to be added.

Potters catered not only for the Corps of Drums of regular and Territorial Army infantry units in Britain, but supplied 'Premier' drums emblazoned at Aldershot to parts of the Australian army, the Canadian army and other overseas regiments. They had a good business too in heraldic regalia for the army of the United States including the President's own band, and Marine Corps band, in Washington. And it was this kind of activity which superseded the manufacture of military drums after the adoption of rod-tensioning for which small workshops like theirs had neither the finance nor the expertise. A modern *factory* was now required for the technically more sophisticated production methods, with die-castings and the rest.

Drum-making had ceased to be a craft. Any small workshop could produce rope-tensioned drums, and there were many of them apart from Henry Potter and George Potter such as Hebblewhite and Boosey & Hawkes, who competed for Ordnance contracts right up to the introduction of rod-tensioning in the 1950s. But it was now a different ball game. David Leech had no regrets.

I see our activity to-day as akin to that of the coachbuilder of the past who were master craftsmen in the art of embellishment. And we are busier doing this than we ever were as manufacturers – and we continue to make the Fifes with Five keys which are the flutes used by Corps of Drums.

I welcomed rod-tensioning as giving a new boost to the whole trade. Apart from reducing maintenance to a minimum, rod-tensioning plus a plastic head produced what I consider an improved tone which remained even and consistent however hard it rained. As the years have gone by, the technical advances in the production of drums have been considerable. Now drums are designed for particular military groupings. For instance, there is one type for a Scottish Pipe Band pitched high to accompany bagpipes (tuned to A), another to be beaten with bugles and flutes. Drums tensioned to 150 pounds a square inch on plastic heads have the usual shape but, with their armour plating of the material used to make bullet-proof vests, they have a different weight and a different look. And now there is something in the pipeline called a 'Legato' drum, hailing from Australia I think, which will dispense with our kind of tension rods altogether. What that will sound and look like only time will tell.

Whatever its pitch, whatever its look, one thing is certain. The imperative, gut-tearing, primaeval ta-pum of the military drum remains. It has been untouched by the changes of the centuries, and is surely destined to transcend whatever more may lie ahead – beating Time at its own game?

George Potter & Co
of Aldershot –
yesterday and to-day.

APPENDIX

ARMY DRUMMERS
who have been awarded
THE VICTORIA CROSS

Drummer M Ryan, *1st European Bengal Fusiliers*, Indian Mutiny, 14 September 1857

Drummer T Flinn, *64th Regiment*, Indian Mutiny, 28 November 1857

Drummer D Stagpoole, *57th Regiment*, New Zealand, 2 October 1863

Drummer M Magner, *33rd Regiment*, Abyssinia, 13 April 1868

Drummer S J Bent, *1st Battalion East Lancashire Regiment*, near Le Gheer, Belgium,
    2 November 1914

Drummer W Kenny, *2nd Battalion Gordon Highlanders*, near Ypres, Belgium,
    23 November 1914

Drummer W Ritchie, *2nd Battalion Seaforth Highlanders*, north of Beaumont Hamel,
    France, 1 July 1916

The date is that of the award-winning deed, not the date of gazette.

The Victoria Cross was instituted in 1856, but made retrospective to the autumn
of 1854.

LIST OF ILLUSTRATIONS

IN COLOUR

IN BLACK AND WHITE

Acknowledgements

COLOUR All by courtesy of The National Army Museum, except the Clifford Walton drawings, The Royal United Services Institute; the Alfred Munnings painting the C O, Household Cavalry Regiment; the St David's Day ceremonies, Curator the Royal Welch Fusiliers Museum; the Rembrandt drawing, Trustees of The British Museum; The Connaught Rangers drummer, Peter Walton; pictures by David Morier and N D Finart, by gracious permission of Her Majesty the Queen.

BLACK & WHITE pp 10. 19 The Royal United Services Institute; pp 12, 14, 15, 31, 33, 37, 46, 47, 65, 72, 74, 104 The National Army Museum; p 32 W Y Carman; p 69 Fotomas Index; pp 62, 70, 82 and chapter headings, The Army Museums Ogilby Trust; p 101 Mr W G F Boag; pp 23, 52, 85, 90, 93, 111, 113 Mary Evans Picture Library; pp 27, 28, 42, 120 George Potter & Co.

BIBLIOGRAPHY

The Journal of the Society of Army Historical Research
Coronation of James II, the Grand Proceeding.   no 16 1937
Rev Percy Summer FSA, 'The Regimental Accounts for Clothing and Equipment of the 1st Royal Dragoons 1764 to 1782'.   no 16 1937.
E J Martin (ed), 'Diary of Lieutenant Hamilton Hodgson, The Lincolnshires at Omdurman, September 1898'.   no 16 1937.
G Derbridge, 'A History of the Drums and Fifes 1650 to 1700'.   no 44.
Henry George Farmer PhD, DLitt, 'Turkish Influence in Military Music'
                              'The Martial Fife'.   no 1945.
                              '16th-17th Century Military Marches'.
                              'Kettledrums as Trophies'. vol 26 1948
James Blades, *Percussion Instruments and Their History*, Faber 1970
Major T J Edwards, *Military Customs*, Gale & Polden 1948 (4th ed. 1954)
Francis Grose FAS, *Military Antiquities* respecting a History of the English Army from the Conquest to the Present Time, vol 2, 1786 (1812 ed)
Henry Cart De Lafontaine, *The King's Musick*, A Transcript of Records relating to Music and Musicians 1460-1700, London 1909.
W Y Carman, FIRM, regimental magazine of The Worcestershire Regiment, January 1947, 'The Development of the Drum'; July 1947, 'The Dress of the Drummer'.
Robert Barret, *The Theoricke and Practice of Moderne Warres, Booke 4, 1598*
Captain G R Howe, 2nd Battalion, The Buffs, *Drums and Drummers* Medici Society 1932
                              Manual for the Drums, 1931
Brigadier Peter Young and Wilfrid Emberton, *The Cavalier Army, Its Organisation and Everyday Life*, George Allen & Unwin 1974
Hon J W Fortescue, *A History of the British Army* vol 1, 1910 *The Drummer's Coat*, Macmillan 1900
Lewis Winstock, *Songs and Marches of the Roundheads and Cavaliers* Leo Cooper 1971
Colonel William Barriffe, *Militarie Discipline* or the Young Artillery-Man, London 1661
Joseph Addison, *The Drummer, or the Haunted House*, 1792
Captain Thomas Venn, *Military and Maritime Discipline*, 1672
The Queen's Hussars Tercentenary Edition 1685-1985
Major J E R Bulkeley, 'The Drum Horse Ensemble'
Major L J Melhuish, 'Dettingen'
Drummers Call no 1 April 1978
             no 19, Winter 1982/3 'Duties of a Drum Major 1875'
             no 24, Spring 1984, 'Minden Day' & 'A Personal Account' by C Gay
             no 25, Spring 1985 'A Matter of Pride' by David Rowlands.
Lieutenant Colonel W H Goodenough & Lieutenant Colonel J C Dalton *The Army Book for the British Empire* 1893
Henry Harris, *The Royal Irish Fusiliers*, Leo Cooper 1972
George Blaxland, *The Middlesex Regiment*, Leo Cooper 1977
Louis Cohen, *Napoleonic Anecdotes*, London 1925
Captain Moyle Sherer, *Recollections of the Peninsula* 3rd ed, London 1824
Samuel Potter, *The Art of Beating the Drum* London 1810

David Scott Daniell, *Cap of Honour,* the story of The Gloucestershire Regiment (28th/61st Foot) 1694-1950, Harrap 1951

Corporal Ryder, *Four Years Service in India,* Leicester 1853 (from *Rank and File*)

R G Harris 'Cavalry Mounted Bands, Drum Horses and Drum Banners', *Military Modelling Magazine* 1983

A E Haswell Miller & N P Dawnay, *Military Drawings & Paintings in the Royal Collection,* vol 2 'Notes'. Phaidon 1966

Infantry Training *The Drummer's Handbook,* Ministry of Defence February 1985 Army Code on 71333.

Major R Money Barnes, *The Soldiers of London* 1963

Rudyard Kipling, *Drums of the Fore and Aft,* Macmillan 1888.

Private E C Moffet, *With the Eighth Division: A Souvenir of the South African Campaign* 1903 (from *Rank and File*)

One of their Medical Officers [Captain C J Dunn], The Royal Welch Fusiliers, *The Warfare the Infantry Knew 1914-1919* London 1938

Major L M Wilson *Regimental Music of the Queen's Regiment* 1980

Joshua Sprigge MA, *Anglia Rediviva:* England's Recovery, being the History of the Motions, Actions and Successes of the Army under the Immediate Conduct of His Excellency Sir Thomas Fairfax Kt, Captain-General of all the Parliamentary Forces in England, 1647

Major-General R H Whitworth, *The Grenadier Guards,* Leo Cooper 1974

David Ascoli, *A Companion to the British Army* 1660-1983, Harrap 1983

Colonel Clifford Walton CB, Assistant Adjutant General, *History of the British Standing Army 1660-1700, London 1894*

C H Firth, *Cromwell's Arms,* Methuen 1902 (4th ed 1962)

Jack Cassin-Smith and John Fabb, *Military Bands and Their Uniforms,* Blandford 1978

Sir George Grove, *Grove's Dictionary of Music and Musicians,* 1879-99.

Colonel Cleaveland RA, *Notes on the Early History of the Royal Regiment of Artillery* London 1880

Henry George Farmer Ph D, D Litt, *The Rise and Development of Military Music,* 1912
          Memoirs of the Royal Artillery Band, 1904
          British Bands in Battle, Hinrichsen no 1482

Robert Ward, Gentleman and Commander, *Animadversions of Warre,* 1639

Francis Markham, *Five Decades of Epistles of Warre,* 1622

Sir John Hawkins, *A General History of the Science and Practice of Music,* vol 2 1776

T H McGuffie (ed), *Rank and File,* the Common Soldier at Peace and War 1642-1914, Hutchinson 1964

Thomas Simes, *The Military Medley* 1768
          A Military Course for the Government and Conduct of a Battalion, 1768

Lieutenancy of London Minute Book 2 December 1714 to 18 October 1744

Major R E Scouller, *The Armies of Queen Anne* Oxford University press 1966

Anon, *Cautions and Advices to Officers of the Army, particularly Subalterns* Edinburgh 1777.

J Shipp, *Memoirs of the Military Career of John Shipp* 1843 (from *Rank and File*)

Pryse Lockhart Gordon, *Personal Memoris* 1830

INDEX

Middlesex Regiment, The 83
Militia 26, 45, 51-2, 74-5
Minden Day 68
Moffet, Pte E C *quoted* 106
Monk, Gen George (1st Duke of
    Albemarle) 26, 35
Mons, Retreat from 109-10
Mordaunt, Capt John 25-6

nakers 30, 37
Napoleon I (Bonaparte) 79-80, 84
Newbolt, Sir Henry *quoted* 109-10

Old English March 21-2
Omdurman, Battle of 105-6

Parley 16, 20, 44
parleying 15-7, 32
Peninsular War 83-4
Pepys, Samuel *quoted* 18, 23
Pope, Alexander *quoted* 105
Potter (drum makers) 66, 86-9, 90, 96-8,
    99, 103, 105
Potter, Henry 118
Potter, Major J G R 118
Potter, Samuel 86-8, 103
Powell, Richard *quoted* 95
Premier Percussion Ltd. 118
Preparative 12, 13, 47
Prince of Wales's Own Regiment of
    Yorkshire: *see* West Yorkshire
    Regiment
punishment duties 36, 53-4, 91

Queen's Own Buffs: *see* Buffs
Queen's Own Hussars, The 66-7
Queen's Regiment, The 115; *see also* Buffs;
    Middlesex Regiment; Queen's Royal
    Regiment
Queen's Royal Lancers: *see* Royal Irish
    Lancers
Queen's Royal Regiment, The 18

Raglan, FM Lord 93-94
recruiting 25, 58-61, 112
Regimental Drum-Major 12, 50, 73
Retreat (Drum Call) 13, 14, 24, 47, 87, 100
Reveille (Revally) 24, 47, 87, 113
Rifle Regiments 92
rod-tensioning 117-9, 118
Rogues March 54
rolls 23, 64, 86-7, 95

rope-tensioning 117, 118
Royal Anglian Regiment, The 109; *see also*
    Lincolnshire Regiment Royal
    Artillery: *see* Artillery, Royal
    Regiment of
Royal Berkshire Regiment, The 95
Royal East Kent Regiment; *see* Buffs
Royal Fusiliers: See Fusiliers, Royal
Royal Highland Fusiliers: *see* Royal Scots
    Fusiliers
Royal Horse Guards, The 63-4, 97
Royal Irish Fusiliers, The 81-82, 106
Royal Irish Lancers, The 96
Royal Marines 26, 116, 118
Royal Northumberland Fusiliers, The 68-
    9, 95, 108
Royal Scots Fusiliers, The 93
Royal Welch Fusiliers, The 110-1
Russell, (Sir) William *quoted* 93-4
Ryder, Cpl *quoted* 90-1

St Cas 67
St Quentin 33, 39
Saracens 30-1
Scots Guards 106, 116
Scots March 23
Scottish Regiments 92-3, 112-4
Scottish United Services Museum, 118
Second World War 67, 114
Sedgemoor, Battle of 18
Sergeant-Drummer 94, 107-8
Shakespeare, William *quoted* 32, 34
shakos 83
Sherer, Capt Moyle *quoted* 83-4
Shields, F J 72
Shortis, Maj-Gen C T *quoted* 115
Shipp, John 75; *quoted* 59, 73
side-drummers/side-drums 23, 24, 30, 33,
    34, 37-8, 40-1, 44, 89, 105, 107, 109,
    112, 113, 116
Simes, Thomas *quoted* 45-6, 47-8, 49, 53,
    55-6
Smollett, Tobias *quoted* 64, 65, 67
Somme, Battle of the 110
South African War: *see* Boer War
Sprigge, Joshua *quoted* 17
staffs (Drum-Major's) 35, 94, 95, 97, 108
Stagpoole, Drummer D 100
Steady the Drums and Fifes. 83
Stow, John *quoted* 32

tabo(u)rs 30, 32, 33, 38
Tarifa, Battle of 82

Tattoo (Taptoo) 24, 47, 87, 100
Tattoos (events) 100, 113
tenor drummers/drums 89, 97, 107, 113, 116
Tidworth (Tedworth) 18, 20
Troop (Drum Call) 12, 25, 47, 87
Turkish music 29-31, 40, 88, 89
Turner, Sir James *quoted* 38-9

Venn, Capt Thomas *quoted* 12-3, 24
Victoria, Queen 90, 94
Victoria Cross 100

Waller, Sir William 20
Walton, Col Clifford 36
Ward, Cornelius 88, 99, 118
Ward, Robert 35; *quoted* 16, 17

Warlike Directions 21
Waterloo, Battle of 84, 89, 99
Wellington, Duke of, 118
Wentworth, Col Lord 26
West Yorkshire Regiment, The 81, 109, 117
Wilhelmstahl, Battle of 68-9
Westminster Dragoons 91
Winstock, Lewis quoted *23*
Worcestershire and Sherwood Foresters Regiment:
   see *Worcestershire Regiment*
Worcestershire Regiment, The 57, 63, 114
World War I: see *Great War*
World War II: see *Second World War*

Yeomanry 99